D0558705

AMERICAN INSTITUTE FOR ECONOMIC RESEARCH

CORONAVIRUS
AND
ECONOMIC
CRISIS

EDITED BY
PETER C. EARLE

ISBN: 9781630692001

Cover art: Vanessa Mendozzi

CORONAVIRUS

AND

ECONOMIC CRISIS

EDITED BY

PETER C. EARLE

AIER | AMERICAN INSTITUTE
for ECONOMIC RESEARCH

CONTENTS

CRISIS AND CHAOS   111

INTRODUCTION

The conventional wisdom, still coalescing as of this writing, is that the American coronavirus experience officially began on January 21, 2020; on that day, the US Centers for Disease Control and Prevention announced that the first domestic case had been discovered in Washington State. For roughly five weeks, news of an escalating health crisis in Wuhan Province had been leaking out of China—much of it surreptitiously reported via anonymous social media accounts. It was not long before the inevitability of the disease's spread became clear, and less than a week after the disease had reached the US, the American Institute for Economic Research's first article on the uncoiling pandemic appeared, with many more to follow.

In those opening days of what soon became an international emergency of historic proportions, AIER's researchers swung into action: devouring reports, discussing rapidly changing facts and political developments, analyzing historical precedents and new developments, and writing. We wrote, quite literally, around the clock—from late nights, to early mornings, to rushed and skipped meals. It was a ceaseless cycle of taking down each new report and idea, editing one another's work, fact-checking, and often revising until moments before publication.

During that time, we noted that there was a desperate need for other voices besides the mainstream media, which flew into an overdrive state of panic. There needs to be an independent voice, but few others were writing about the virus, and certainly not about the probable (and later realized) policy responses, much less their likely financial, economic, and social impact. AIER stepped up.

The willingness to speak up early—and thus often alone, at least initially—speaks directly to the institutional DNA of the American Institute for Economic Research. We were founded in 1933 by a young, intellectually curious Army officer who felt duty-bound to respond to the growing academic capture in economic policy making, and in particular the politicization of monetary policy. His writings under the auspices of AIER, completely consistent with his commissioning oath, aroused the ire of higher-ups in the Roosevelt administration, resulting in investigations and threats by agents and officials in the War Department.

Clearly stated in our Articles of Association (1939), AIER exists

> so that there may be more widespread understanding of the fundamental economic relationships affecting the citizens of the United States, both as individuals and as members of a complex economic society, with the ultimate object of advancing the welfare of the American people.

Closing in on ninety years later, the researchers and staff of AIER once again find ourselves in the midst of a rapidly evolving morass with few proponents of free markets by our side.

In the weeks after the virus began to spread within the United States, waves of fear-mongering and appeals to swift, heavy government intervention inundated the major news networks. By March 11, when the World Health Organization had officially classified the spread of the coronavirus a pandemic, a run on supermarkets had already begun. Over the next ten days, numerous allusions were made to World War II, and the president of the United States invoked the Defense Production Act. The stock market crashed for the first time in thirty-three years, experiencing its second worst day in a century in a one-day decline more severe than either of the two days of the Crash of '29.

Around the world, polities on six continents ranging from tiny municipalities to entire nations quarantined nearly one billion citizens, imposed curfews and travel bans, deployed their militaries, and crushed the private sector. (To date, South Korea and Singapore represent the lone recusants from that trend.)

And thus a mere forty days after the first case of COVID-19 was reported in the US, even before rates of transmission or recovery could be accurately calculated, plans were in motion for over $4 trillion in government stimulus and bailout packages. Central banks unleashed a torrent of programs, flooding the world economy with money. And even at this point, the American Institute for Economic Research was still nearly alone in bringing liberal ideas and analysis to bear on the unfolding calamity.

The contributions of every economist and thinker in the liberal tradition have been vindicated throughout what are likely only the beginnings of this disaster: Menger's and Fetter's work on the subjective theory of value, which informed both the actions of individuals who acquired goods in advance and the prices that were later offered by people desperate to acquire them. The warnings of Hayek with respect to the pretense of knowledge, and of Morgenstern regarding the questionable accuracy of statistics in the social sciences. Ludwig von Mises' observation that government intervention always results in further interventions owing to the unintended consequences of the first round of tinkering. And our own E. C. Harwood's encouragement to be bold in the defense of liberty along with his counsel that "for integrity, there is no substitute."

This book chronicles AIER's coverage of the opening phase of the world coronavirus outbreak, through the full onset of the crisis, with speculations on the future of wealth and liberty in light of both the virus and the political response.

Special thanks are due to Micha Gartz, Alexander Gleason, and David Schatz for remarkable copyediting and other work on this. Jeffrey Tucker conceived of the project and led editorial direction during the crisis. AIER's president Edward Stringham, who was on television almost daily in these weeks, has provided non-stop support. Finally, my wife Mary, a brilliant and dedicated medical professional who is right now tending to coronavirus patients, is my endless source of support and inspiration and the person to whom I dedicate my labors on this book.

May this book serve as important documentation of what this country and the world can learn for the future.

Peter C. Earle
March 20, 2020

BEFORE THE CRISIS

THE UNDERAPPRECIATED TREND IN MORTALITY AND INEQUALITY
BY VINCENT GELOSO

February 19, 2020.

Most economists, left or right, care about human development. By human development, they mean more than simply increases in income. They refer to a greater ability for individuals to choose the lives they deem most fulfilling under continually weakening constraints.[1] Regardless of their political leanings, most economists will also be concerned with the inequalities in human development.

This sort of inequality is hard to measure. Generally, we concentrate on income inequality to measure those inequalities. This tends to create false impressions about how unequal the world has grown since the early 19th century. In fact, numerous indicators suggest that the world is now more equal than it was in the past!

Concentrating solely on incomes is bound to have shortcomings. The issue with income is that the levels capture both opportunities available to workers and the decisions they make. For example, it is well-known that after a certain wage level, workers will use wage increases to substitute leisure for paid work time.

This is known as the backward bending labor supply curve. However, the curve is not the same for everyone. Some workers simply decide

---

1 Phelps, Edmund. 2013. Mass *Flourishing: How Grassroots Innovation Created Jobs, Challenge, and Change*. Princeton University Press: Princeton, NJ; Sen, Amartya. "Development as Freedom." *OUP Catalogue*, Oxford University Press. Number 9780192893307.

to work more than others (or have incentives to do so).[2] This is why we observe rising inequality in *working hours* in richer countries.[3] In a situation like this, how can we assess the inequality in human development (i.e. inequality in our ability to make choices)?

Measures such as the human development index (HDI) use a broader set of indicators to capture human development.[4] One such indicator is life expectancy at birth. It is taken as a proxy for how healthy our lives are. The intuition is that the healthier we are, the more we are able to make choices. If life expectancy at birth can be taken as a reliable indicator of health outcomes broadly defined, inequalities in life expectancy will be relevant to inequality in human development.

What do such measures say? Using demographic data accessible to all, Sam Peltzman made the exercise of measuring inequality in life expectancy in a 2009 article in the *Journal of Economic Perspectives*.[5] He calculated the Gini coefficient for that indicator since the late 19th century for many countries and as far back as 1750 for a few countries such as Sweden and Germany. The Gini coefficient takes a value of zero if there is perfect equality and a value of one if there is perfect inequality.

What does his exercise yield? The Gini coefficient for Sweden,

2 Lemieux, Thomas, W. Bentley MacLeod & Daniel Parent. 2009. "Performance Pay and Wage Inequality." *The Quarterly Journal of Economics*, 124(1): 1-49.

3 Gerold, Stefanie & Ulrike Stein. 2018. "Inequality of working hours, income inequality, and the role of collective bargaining in Germany."

4 UNDP. "Human Development Index (HDI)." *United Nations Development Program*, Human Development Reports.

5 Peltzman, Sam. 2009. "Morality Inequality." *Journal of Economic Perspectives*, 23(4): 175-190.

England, France, Germany and the United States stood between 0.4 and 0.5 for most of the 19th century. However, there was a clear downward trend in mortality inequality so that by 1900, the level had fallen to a range between 0.3 and 0.4. By 1950, the drop had continued and stood instead between 0.1 and 0.2. Today it is closer to 0.1. Similar declines are observed in countries like India, Brazil and Japan over the course of the 20th century.

In fact, Peltzman points out that in some countries like India and Brazil, "mortality is distributed more than income." This is a momentous collapse in the inequality in life expectancy. Peltzman made a similar exercise using life expectancy for American states starting in 1910 and found a marked decline in life expectancy inequality within the United States.

What used to be a major source of inequality is now a minor source of inequality in human development. The unhealthy focus on income inequality makes us blind to these great developments in human well-being. This is not to say that analysis of income (or wealth) inequality should be abandoned. However, it ought to be complemented with other indicators of inequality. A great number of indicators would constitute a dashboard for sober analysis. At the very least, it would give us the capacity to appreciate how we are living in a more equal and richer world than we used to before.

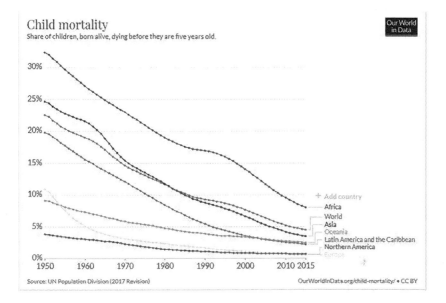

Child mortality
Share of children, born alive, dying before they are five years old.

Our World in Data

- Add country
- Africa
- World
- Asia
- Oceania
- Latin America and the Caribbean
- Northern America
- Europe

Source: UN Population Division (2017 Revision)

OurWorldInData.org/child-mortality/ • CC BY

THE ECONOMICS OF PANDEMICS AND QUARANTINES
BY VINCENT GELOSO

January 28, 2020.

News out of Wuhan in China generated a wave of fears regarding the spread of the coronavirus. Public health organizations issued guidelines on how to minimize risks of infection and China's government took the drastic step of sealing off Wuhan.

The story is unfolding in a manner very similar to the Ebola outbreak a few years back. Authorities react with strong measures such as quarantines and travel bans to restrict contagion. On its face, such measures appear—purely from the vantage point of public health issues—reasonable. However, economic theory suggests the possibility that extreme measures such as sealing off a city, a travel ban or quarantines may actually make things worse.

First, it is necessary to point that pandemics have, since the 19th century, fallen in importance. For example, a 2006 article in *Emerging Infectious Diseases* compared the influenza epidemics of 1918, 1951, 1957 and 1968 in England, Wales, Canada and the United States and found that death rates at each outbreak kept falling relative to the previous one.[6]

Using a longer time horizon that has some uncertainties about case fatalities, a 2001 article in the *Journal of Applied Microbiology* documents a rapid collapse in influenza-related deaths (which

---

6 Viboud C, Tam T, Fleming D, Miller M A, Simonsen L. 2006. "1951 Influenza Epidemic, England and Wales, Canada, and the United States." *Emerging Infectious Diseases*, 12(4): 661–668.

when combined with population figures suggests a faster collapse in death rates).[7] Other articles find that, since the 1950s, death rates from different strains of influenza have stabilized at historically low levels in spite of the fact that we live in a world with more travel, more exchange and more social connections (i.e. more chances to transmit infectious diseases).[8]

And these numbers speak only to influenza. Deaths from other forms of infectious diseases are at historically low levels if they have not disappeared entirely.[9] Thus, it is necessary to place the current situation in a historical context. This does not invalidate the idea that there are serious costs from currently observed pandemics: estimates place this figure at 0.6% of global income which is not a trivial figure—especially in lower-income countries where the costs are more than twice as high.[10]

But why could quarantines and travel bans be problematic? The answer is that it all boils down to how people affected by the public health policy responses perceive costs. Consider the following thought experiment constructed by Alice Mesnard and Paul Seabright in the

---

7 Potter, C. W. 2008. "A history of Influenza." *Journal of Applied Microbiology,* 91: 572-579.

8 Taubenberger, Jeffrey K, John C Kash, David M Morens. 2019. "The 1918 influenza pandemic: 100 years of questions answered and unanswered." *Science Translational Medicine,* 11(502).

9 Madhav N, Oppenheim B, Gallivan M, et al. 2017. Chapter 17: "Pandemics: Risks, Impacts, and Mitigation." In *Disease Control Priorities: Improving Health and Reducing Poverty,* 3[re] Ed. Washington DC: The World Bank; and Ochmann, Sophie, Max Roser. 2020. "Smallpox." *OurWorldInData.org.*

10 Fan, Victoria Y, Dean T Jamison, Lawrence H Summers. 2018. "Pandemic risk: how large are the expected losses?" *World Health Organization,* December 5.

Journal of Public Economics.[11] People who live in areas with high prevalence of infectious diseases face costs in the form of higher risks of infection. Thus, the uninfected who understand accurately their own infection status stand to gain from migrating away. As a result, they implicitly quarantine the disease and reduce the potential for contagion. This is what Mesnard and Seabright call "first best."

However, if individuals at risk are uncertain of their infection status (i.e. they either contracted the disease but are still unaware of it or they are uninfected), their decision to migrate can allow the disease to spread. The hiccup comes from these individuals existing in a setting of imperfect information. If a quarantine is applied, those at-risk individuals are stuck with the already infected. This increases their perception of costs and, by definition, leads to investing more in trying to migrate. If they are unaware that they are already sick but manage to escape the quarantine area, they spread the disease. Thus, a quarantine that is too extreme induces a behavioral response to more aggressively attempt to escape the quarantine. In the end, this may increase infection rates.

This potential backfire of public health measures suggests the possibility that milder measures might be cheaper and more effective in containing infectious diseases. For example, one article in *PlosOne* studied purchased flights that were missed by passengers in relation to news trends regarding infectious diseases.[12] In other words, the people who missed their flights because they feared infections. This

---

11 Mesnard, Alice, Paul Seabright. 2009. "Escaping epidemics through migration? Quarantine measures under incomplete information about infection risk." *Journal of Public Economics*, 93(7-8): 931-938.

12 Fenichel, Eli P., Nicolai V Kuminoff, Gerardo Chowell. 2013. "Skip the Trip: Air Travelers' Behavioral Responses to Pandemic Influenza." *PLoS One,* 8(3): 1-10.

defensive move on the part of private individuals came at a cost of $50 million over two years. The same study found however that news sources were highly inaccurate in depicting *actual* infectious cases, but people still responded to media reactions.

The authors of the paper point out that had passengers responded to actual cases of infections rather than news scares, the cost of $50 million could have been reduced to half that figure. This suggests that clearer risk communication could improve people's understanding of their constraints. As such, individuals self-quarantine themselves and reduce the risks of contracting the disease.

The contrast provided above suggests that soft-handed measures are cheaper and more effective in diminishing contagion than heavy-handed measures. This is something worth bearing in mind as news keeps unfolding about the reaction of authorities in China to the outbreak of the coronavirus.

MUST GOVERNMENT SAVE US FROM THE CORONAVIRUS
BY JEFFREY TUCKER

January 27, 2020.

In the spring of 2014, when awareness of Ebola was just beginning to dawn, a case of infection appeared in the town of Harbel, Liberia. The biggest employer in the area is Firestone. The company immediately set up a quarantine area of its hospital for the infected woman, who soon died.

They distributed hazmat suits to workers. They researched everything they could, built a treatment center, and set up a comprehensive response. Transmission stopped. Even now, the only cases seen in this area come from outside the community.

National Public Radio reported on the case and concluded:[13]

> even as the worst Ebola outbreak ever recorded rages all around them, Firestone appears to have blocked the virus from spreading inside its territory… A key reason for Firestone's success is the close monitoring of people who have potentially been exposed to the virus — and the moving of anyone who has had contact with an Ebola patient into voluntary quarantine. By most accounts, this Ebola outbreak remains out of control, with health care workers across West Africa struggling to contain it.

Another triumph of the market and human volition! Still, somehow,

---

13 Beaubien, Jason. 2014. "Firestone Did What Governments Have Not: Stopped Ebola In Its Tracks." *NPR*, October 6.

the lesson here has not penetrated. As with every crisis in the history of the modern world, Ebola fears gave rise to debates over government power, just as the Coronavirus has today.

China has kicked into gear the largest quarantine in modern history. As George E. Wantz, distinguished professor of the history of medicine at the University of Michigan, has written:[14]

> To combat the contagion, the Chinese government has taken the extraordinary step of quarantining the city of Wuhan, as well as neighboring districts and cities. The borders are sealed, and all transportation out is blocked. Officials closed the public transportation systems. Friday morning, more than 35 million people woke up facing aggressive curtailments of their freedom.

Is all this necessary? Wantz looks at the numbers:

> It's possible that this coronavirus may not be highly contagious, and it may not be all that deadly. We also do not know yet how many people have mild coronavirus infections but have not come to medical attention, especially because the illness begins with mild to moderate respiratory tract symptoms, similar to those of the common cold, including coughing, fever, sniffles and congestion. Based on data from other coronaviruses, experts believe the incubation period for this new coronavirus is about five days (the range runs from two to 14 days), but we do not yet know how efficiently this coronavirus spreads from infected

14 Markel, Howard. 2020. "Be wary of China's coronavirus quarantine." *The Washington Post*, January 24.

person to healthy person. And because antibodies for coronavirus do not tend to remain in the body all that long, it is possible for someone to contract a "cold" with coronavirus and then, four months later, catch the virus again.

The case fatality rate, a very important statistic in epidemiology, is calculated by dividing the number of known deaths by the number of known cases. At present, the virus appears to have a fatality rate of about 3%, which mirrors that of the influenza pandemic of 1918. But what if there are 100,000 Chinese citizens in Wuhan with mild infections that we do not know about? That would lower the case fatality rate to a mere 0.02%,which comes closer to seasonal flu death rates. If that's the case, a major disruption like the Chinese quarantine would seem foolish and cost a fortune in terms of public health efforts, interrupted commerce, public dissonance, trust, good will and panic.

In sum, this virus might be as serious as any seasonal flu or it might be much worse. There are still too many unknowns. Still, when people are afraid, they have this irrational penchant for reaching out to government to save them. Never mind that the power might be abused or might not even be a necessary, much less suitable, power. Government is magic: if something is big, important, or crucial, people long for government to do it.

Do we need a Coronavirus Czar, operating under the Department of Homeland Security and the National Security Adviser? These are the same people who spy on your email, record your phone calls, watch your online habits, run the TSA security theater, and so on. What does any of this have to do with health? No one can doubt that the Coronavirus will be used, just like every real crisis before it, as a means of amping up government power.

The thinking goes like this. The virus is terrifying. We can't just allow people to wander around with the disease and infect others. We could all die under those conditions. So we need government to discern who has the disease, force these people against their will to stay away from others, and even put together a plan for how to deal with a mass outbreak, even if that involves creating camps of sick people and keeping them all there by force.

The US government already has an extensive plan for dealing with communicable diseases, and these plans involve forcible quarantines. You can read all about it at the website for the Centers for Disease Control.

> Regulations prescribed under this section may provide for the apprehension and examination of any individual reasonably believed to be infected with a communicable disease in a qualifying stage and (A) to be moving or about to move from a State to another State; or (B) to be a probable source of infection to individuals who, while infected with such disease in a qualifying stage, will be moving from a State to another State. Such regulations may provide that if upon examination any such individual is found to be infected, he may be detained for such time and in such manner as may be reasonably necessary.

These regulations are enforced, but you might be surprised at the light penalties:

> Any person who violates any regulation prescribed under sections 264 to 266 of this title, or any provision of section 269 of this

title or any regulation prescribed thereunder, or who enters or
departs from the limits of any quarantine station, ground, or
anchorage in disregard of quarantine rules and regulations or
without permission of the quarantine officer in charge, shall be
punished by a fine of not more than $1,000 or by imprisonment
for not more than one year, or both.

So, if you are willing to risk coughing up $1K or going to the pokey
for a year, you can pretty much walk around infected with anything,
and infect anyone else? If that's your goal, it's not likely that such
penalties are going to deter you. I can't imagine that anyone thinks:
"I would like to infect lots of people with my deadly disease but I'm
rethinking it because I just can't afford the $1,000 fine."

In the meantime, the US government already has the power to
create sick camps, kidnap and intern people upon suspicion that they are
diseased, and keep people in camps for an undetermined amount of time.

The Surgeon General shall control, direct, and manage all United
States quarantine stations, grounds, and anchorages, designate
their boundaries, and designate the quarantine officers to be in
charge thereof. With the approval of the President he shall from
time to time select suitable sites for and establish such additional
stations, grounds, and anchorages in the States and possessions
of the United States as in his judgment are necessary to prevent
the introduction of communicable diseases into the States and
possessions of the United States.

Anyone concerned about human freedom should be uncomforta-
ble with this policy, especially given the hysteria that surrounds the

issue of communicable diseases. Rules don't guarantee results, and government has no solid reason to be careful about who gets put into the camps and why. It is easy to imagine a scenario in which such powers end up exposing undiseased people rather than protecting people from the disease.

It's true that quarantine powers have been around since the ancient world and have been invoked through US history from colonial times to the present. They are hardly questioned. I was once in a debate over the role of government and my opponent relied heavily on this power as proof that we need some government—because society is just too stupid to figure out how to deal with such a deadly problem.

On the other hand, abuse of such powers is even more frequent.[15] The problem is the low threshold concerning risk. Once government has the power, it can use it anyway it wants. In World War I, prostitutes were routinely arrested and quarantined in the name of preventing the spread of diseases. In the 1892 typhus outbreak, it became common to arrest and quarantine any immigrant from Russia, Italy, or Ireland even without any evidence of disease.

And it's not just about disease. The quarantine power has been used by despotic governments all over the world to round up political enemies under the thinnest excuse. Fear of disease is as good an excuse as any. For a complete list of concentration and internment camps, see this Wikipedia entry.[16]

---

15 Kourinian, Arsen. 2010. "A History of Abuse and Lack of Protection: The Need to Update California 's Quarantine Powers in Light of the H1N1 Influenza Outbreak." *Loyola of Los Angeles Law Review*, 43(2):693-710.

16 *Wikipedia*. 2020. "List of concentration and internment camps." *Wikipedia,* March 19.

Is it really true that government needs quarantine power? Let's think rationally and normally about this. Imagine that you are feeling not-so-great. You go to the hospital and it is discovered that you have a deadly communicable disease. Are you going anywhere? No. It's preposterous. These days, you can't even go to the office with a cough without eliciting the disdain from your fellow employees. I let out a slight cough the other day in a security line and found myself with a five-foot gap between myself and the people in front of and behind me!

Once a deadly disease is discovered, no one has any reason to have the attitude that one should just let it go, embrace death, and take others with you. It only takes a moment of reflection to realize this. You want to be where you can get well or at least minimize pain. If that means staying in isolation, so it is. Even if you don't like this idea, others will make sure that you do understand.

Let's say you just can't stand it. You leap from the window and run. Truly, the whole of the social order would be organized against you, even in the absence of the use of coercion. You would stand no chance of getting so much as a place to sleep or a bite to eat from anyone, anywhere. And, in the real world, such a person is likely to be shot on sight.

Government power is not necessary in any respect. It is not likely to be effective, either. And when it is not effective, the tendency is to overreact in the opposite direction, clamping down and abusing, exactly as we've seen with the War on Terror and China's response to this virus, which might be as serious as seasonal flu outbreaks. Still, people assume that government is doing its job, government fails, and then government gets more power and does awful things with it. It's the same story again and again.

Individuals don't like to get others sick. People don't like to get sick. Given this, we have a mechanism that actually works. Society has an ability and power of its own to bring about quarantine-like results without introducing the risk that the State's quarantine power will be used and abused for political purposes.

Remember that it is not government that discovers the disease, treats the disease, keeps diseased patients from wandering around, or otherwise compels sick people to decline to escape their sick beds. Institutions do this, institutions that are part of the social order and not exogenous to it.

CAN THE CORONAVIRUS END THE TRADE WAR?
BY BRUCE YANDLE

February 8, 2020.

A CNN headline read: "China halves tariffs on $75 billion of US Goods as Coronavirus Outbreak Escalates."[17] Once again, it seems, a deadly virus is accelerating a daunting achievement—in this case, one that has frustrated U.S.-China trade negotiators for more than a year.

Bruised by the human tragedies accompanying the coronavirus and the steps taken to control its spread—which have involved clamp downs on the movement of people and products—the Chinese economy is struggling to regain its footing. Estimates of the nation's 2020 GDP growth are being trimmed, and similar, though much lighter, pruning may take place for the U.S. economy.

China's decision to lower the tariffs it earlier imposed on U.S. goods, largely in response to Trump administration tariffs aimed at China, will help refill shelves for Chinese consumers and assist producers as they struggle to regain footing.

At the same time, in a benevolent tit-for-tat response, a sympathetic America may move to make further reductions of U.S. tariffs on Chinese goods. So, while it would be awkward to celebrate, the virus may be inspiring an expansion of the type of free, open, and prosperity-generating trade that the recent trade war has diminished for our two countries. Were this to happen, we would have yet another

---

17 Pham, Sherisse, & Steven Jiang. 2020. "China halves tariffs on $75 billion worth of US goods, as coronavirus outbreak escalates." *CNN Business News*, February 6.

application of an old maxim: It's an evil wind that blows no good.

Viruses have helped to bring institutional change and eventually improve human prospects. Another example is found in the story of the 1948 formation of the Ohio River Sanitation Commission (Orsanco).[18] Long before there was an Environmental Protection Agency or any meaningful federal water pollution control legislation, the multi-state commission was formed in an effort to reduce the discharge of raw sewage and other pollutants into the Ohio River.

Cincinnati led the effort. With its downstream location, the city could not build water treatment facilities fast enough to provide its citizens with safe drinking water. Pittsburgh and other upstream cities, reaching all the way to New York State, were treating the Ohio as an open sewer. Gravity was a low-cost way to handle their waste. Cincinnati was bearing the cost, and there was no way to send a bill to the upstream river users.

But then, the contaminated Ohio became a breeder for the gastro-enteritis virus. And the virus traveled upstream, bringing sickness and hardship to the raw-sewage dischargers. Incentives matter a lot when it comes to public policy, especially when human health is involved. Outbreaks throughout the Ohio watershed brought a public response. Orsanco was born, the Ohio River began to be treated as an asset instead of a liability, and the commission still flourishes. Among other actions, Orsanco imposed discharge limitations, installed robot monitors throughout the river, and coordinated a renewal of the river's health as well as the health of the people who lived near it.

Coronavirus is imposing horrible costs on human beings across vast

---

18 2020. *Ohio River Valley Water Sanitation Commission.*

regions of the world. Public health threats always require cooperative political responses. With all that is underway, we can expect to see the top priority—coronavirus containment—take hold, and hopefully very soon. Perhaps the prospects for human prosperity may even improve a little, thanks to a virus-led reduction in the trade wars between the United States and China.

CRISIS
UNFOLDS

THE EFFECT OF THE CORONAVIRUS ON FINANCIAL MARKETS
BY PETER C. EARLE

February 25, 2020.

The 1,031 point drop in the Dow Jones Industrial Average yesterday (February 24, 2020) came as a surprise to many investors and even regular market watchers, especially given the recent record close above 29,000. Yet while the drop was the third largest ever in absolute (point) terms, it only registers tenth by the more relevant, meaningful measure: percentage change for the day—just over -3.5%. By comparison, the October 22, 1987 stock market crash saw the index decline 508 points, nearly 23% in percentage terms.

Another way of gauging the relative severity of a decline in stock prices is to compare them against the regulatory criteria which triggers a halt in trading ("trading curbs" or "circuit breakers"). Although they have changed throughout the years, at present there are three tiers that would trigger a trading halt; they are calculated based upon changes in the S&P 500 index. The first is triggered at a 7% drop (generating a 15-minute pause); the second, at a 13% drop (causing a second 15-minute pause; and the last, at a 20% drop, which would halt trading for the rest of the day (unless the declines occur after 3:25 pm EST).

Comparing the magnitude of today's decline to what the New York Stock Exchange itself views as justifying a brief halt in trading, it registered barely half of the decline to cause the first, 15-minute trading pause.

We should take a sober, dispassionate look at forces acting upon the U.S. financial markets. Headlines indicating a "panic" are vastly overwrought. The futures, which begin to trade outside of cash (regular) market hours, were already deeply negative as American traders began to arrive at their desks. On Monday morning when U.S. equity markets open, Asian markets have already closed (at roughly 2 am EST) and various European equity markets have either just closed or are close to closing.

Thus on Monday mornings, the U.S. market is the last to start trading in the new week and takes cues on the "size" of the down move (a three to four percent decrease, on average, in stock prices) from foreign market indices. Certainly individual companies—airlines, for example—see more severe and sometimes company-specific declines, but a look at the decline in foreign markets is usually instructive.

From the perspective of the weekend news about the coronavirus, Asian and European markets provide strong indications of both price direction and magnitude of decline (gain) owing both to (a) their proximity to the unfolding crisis, and (b) the highly, indeed inextricably, intertwined nature of global markets.

U.S. Treasury yields at various points came close to record lows—bond yields move in the opposite direction of their prices—as investors exiting equity markets sought liquid, low-risk assets to park funds in for a while.[19] (Gold, additionally, hit a seven-year high.)

Some of the market commentary hinted at an apocalyptic sentiment, reminiscent of the opening of apocalyptic horror films—the zombie and pandemic genres, specifically. It is a wholly irresponsible, indeed juvenile, perspective. We have seen this before, and came out none the worse for wear.[20]

---

19 La Monica, Paul R. 2020. "Gold at a seven-year high and bond yields flirt with record lows as fear grips Wall Street." *CNN Business*, February 25.

20 White, Martha C. 2020. "SARS wiped $40 billion off world markets; what will coronavirus do?" *NBC News*, January 24.

The sell-off has nothing whatsoever to do with concerns (much less, expectations) of an extinction-level event or some other such cataclysm, however entertaining those are to consider. Stocks—equities—are fundamentally *units of title to aggregates of capital goods*, and financial markets are the social machinery which serves to discount future earnings generated by those aggregates of capital goods. Thus in the most immediate, hysteric-free economic sense, equities were repriced today based upon a consensus expectation of lower earnings in the coming quarters.

Among other valuation methods, one way (a "back-of-envelope" calculation) of determining how fairly priced a stock is has to do with a ratio between the equities price and per-share earnings for the most recent twelve months: the P/E ratio.[21] Increasingly bad news regarding the spread of the coronavirus over the weekend (more cases, in more countries, despite quarantines and other restrictions) led to a swift repricing of Asian and European stocks late Sunday night and early Monday morning, respectively, and in turn to U.S.-listed companies.

That is to say: investors sold stocks, lowering the numerator ("Price") in anticipation—speculating—that the recent news about the coronavirus may give rise to more quarantines; more restrictive measures applied to the international movement of individuals, goods, and services; and most of all: additional uncertainty.

And those changes, they believe, will negatively impact corporate earnings. Stock markets, they say, climb a wall of worry; "up a ladder, but down a slide (chute)." Declines in stock prices typically occur faster and deeper than the upward trudge, for several reasons which behavioral

---

21 Wikipedia. 2019. "Price–earnings ratio." *Wikipedia*, December 13.

finance and other aspects of psychology touch upon. (Suffice it to say: to any investor, and even to corporate insiders, the body of all relevant information regarding a stock's value is at every moment incomplete, unevenly distributed, and subject to instantaneous revision.)

As information trickles out regarding what China knew about the coronavirus, and as speculation about the aggravating effect of ongoing U.S.-China tariffs take shape, more volatility—repricings of stocks all over the world, reflective of both higher and lower expectations where future earnings and growth is concerned—is likely. The interconnected world in which we live, where today I can eat sweet potatoes, tomorrow I can read any of tens of millions of books from around the world, and all the while I'm buying more computer power for less money, works in no small part because of the financial markets' ceaseless weighing and processing of new information.[22]

Via individual traders, large financial institutions, hedge funds, pension funds, and a host of other market participants, world equities markets are "saying:" the newest information we have makes the likelihood of the coronavirus negatively impacting corporate earnings greater. In anticipation of that, prices should come down such that valuations reflect lower earnings. It's not guaranteed, and the next bits of information may result in a complete reversal of that perspective (with a subsequent rise in prices), but this is how it works.

Various legendary investors (Benjamin Graham, Ron McEachern,

---

22 Tucker, Jeffrey A. 2019. "Where Did AOC Get Her Sweet Potatoes?" *American Institute for Economic Research*, February 25; 2020. "Average selling price of desktop personal computers (PCs) worldwide from 2005 to 2015." *Statista*, March 2; Comen, Evan, Michael B. Sauter & Samuel Stebbins. 2020. "The Cost of a Computer the Year You Were Born." *24/7 Wall Street*, January 13.

Warren Buffett) have been credited with saying that in the short term equity markets are a voting machine, but in the long term they act as weighing machines (scales): in every moment of every trading session, the herd effects of a million fears and hopes are at work. But over the long term—years, decades, and generations—how the firm fares under various economic conditions, with changes of management, new technologies and the like present an incrementally clearer view of the value of the firm and its prospects.

An appreciation of markets, in particular free markets in financial instruments which on a tick-by-tick basis marshal and allocate capital on a global scale, requires respect for both the voting machine and the scale.

ECONOMIC POLICY MUST PREPARE FOR PANDEMIC DISEASE
BY PETER C. EARLE AND JEFFREY TUCKER

February 27, 2020.

The prospect of pandemic disease—certainly one with as many unknowns as COVID-19—has a way of focusing one's mind on what matters. Poetically, the turning point for Americans seemed to be Ash Wednesday 2020. That's the day popular culture went from "this is not really a threat at all" to "this could get very serious very fast and change everything."

Ashes to ashes indeed.

At the prospect of mass death by disease, all the strange obsessions that consume the political class—from the need to pillage billionaires to the burning desire to flatten trade deficits—tend to fade in priority.

When the leading medical reporter for *The New York Times* admits that he is stockpiling food and masks, you know that something is getting serious.[23]

It was not even a month ago when AIER presented something most people do not know: the government right now claims to possess totalitarian powers in dealing with pandemic disease.[24] People tweeted that we were being alarmist. Meanwhile, yesterday, on Ash Wednesday, the president refused to rule out using China-like tactics in dealing with COVID-19, including the quarantining of whole cities.

Whoa.

---

23 2020. "The Coronavirus Goes Global." *The New York Times*, Podcast, February 27.

24 See article herein entitled "Must Government Save Us from the Coronavirus?"

The economic impact of something like this could be devastating. Supply chains disrupted. Travel truncated and, in some regions, effectively stopped. Shipments of food and medicine sitting on docks. Workers holed up in apartments for months at a time. And this isn't just about what government demands you do. It is what people are willing to do to limit their exposure. When it comes to life and death, people can become rather risk averse very quickly. They can panic in uncontrollable ways.

Companies are already starting to suspend international travel.[25] Brick-and-mortar stores could get hit with fears of people unwilling to be out in public mixing it up with strangers. This could profoundly affect restaurants, entertainment, commercial conventions, sporting events, concerts, the entire tourism industry, among many other implications. The toy industry is already a disaster in the making.[26]

We're already seeing the effect on financial markets. What will this do to retail prices? We could be looking at some wild and unpredictable swings. Already, 60% of global productivity is dependent on international trade, and that's just what we can see. What we do not see are the infinitely complex ways that productive structures depend on smoothly functioning markets that could all face deep disruption.

Efforts to examine the possible economic impact are few but a 2006 Congressional Budget Office study suggested that a 1918-style pandemic today could drop GDP by 4.25%, which would put the

---

25 Chen, Te-Ping, Saabira Chaudhuri & Rachel Feintzeig. 2020. "Nestlé Halts All Business Travel Abroad as Other Firms Curb Asia, Italy Trips." *The Wall Street Journal*, February 26.

26 Ziobro, Paul. 2020. "Coronavirus Upends Global Toy Industry." *The Wall Street Journal*, February 27.

economy in painful recession territory.

The policy response so far has focused on local governments begging for more money to prepare. Reports the WSJ:[27]

> Meanwhile, New York Gov. Andrew Cuomo is seeking additional state preparedness funds. Connecticut officials said the state may face a shortfall of medical gloves and masks. California municipalities, including San Francisco and San Diego, have issued emergency declarations to prepare for a possible outbreak.

Here's a better idea to consider: cut taxes, tariffs, and any other barriers to commerce and trade immediately and dramatically. This is not a good time for artificial barriers to persist. Tear them down immediately. This is not artificial stimulus. This is what we should do anyway, it's just that the prospect of disease-inspired recession should focus the mind on good policy. This is a much better path than loose monetary policy or more fiscal stimulus, neither of which holds much promise of keeping goods and services in production and trading.

Additionally, prices for essentials (masks, at present) must be allowed to rise without being decried (or prosecuted) as "gouging," in order to ensure that production is directed in areas where profits are highest, thereby raising supply to meet demand.[28]

At present, the U.S. has imposed some $50 billion in tariffs on Chinese imports, while prompting $112 billion in retaliatory tariffs.

27 Morath, Eric & Harriet Torry. 2020. "U.S. Coronavirus Outbreak Would Pose Risk to Record Expansion." *The Wall Street Journal*, February 27.

28 Matsakis, Louise. 2020. "As Covid-19 Spreads, Amazon Tries to Curb Mask Price Gouging." *Wired*, February 25.

States are usually the last to see crises materialize, and all too often their responses exacerbate a crisis, create new crises, or both. The best that can be done in the face of virulent diseases, natural disasters, and other catastrophes is for governments to get out of the way; policywise, first and foremost.

Another thing we can do—also what we should be doing anyway—is promote the spread of liberty. The totalitarian government of China, where the coronavirus pandemic began, hid information and misled outside observers until it became impossible to.

To maintain the illusion of state omniscience, many more people both inside and outside of China will have died than otherwise, and immeasurable global economic damage inflicted as well. And it should be lost upon no one that the highly probable source of the coronavirus—eating what might best and most politely be referred to as exotic animals outside of normal human consumption—occurred in China, where over 150 million people are malnourished.

The prospect of quarantine or other forms of legal impositions can demotivate information flows at a time when they are most necessary. It can also promote a kind of paranoia: what is it that we do not know? There are also human-rights implications, obviously. There is nothing Constitutional about walling off a whole city and forcing everyone to be exposed. It also won't do any good under genuinely pandemic conditions. It could even cause widespread panic.

The best approach to a shocking event like a global pandemic disease with a high death rate is to free the markets and eliminate barriers to trade as soon as possible. This would at least minimize the damage, get goods and services to those who need them, calm the panic, and reward traders and investors for maintaining normalcy and growth insofar as it is possible.

The situation with COVID-19 is already serious and could get worse quickly. We should also get serious about a viable policy response that protects health, liberty, property, peace, and prosperity in bad times.

THE CORONAVIRUS REVEALS THE LIMITS OF MONETARY POLICY
BY JAMES L. CATON

March 2, 2020.

There is a growing buzz in the media that the Federal Reserve and other central banks should provide support due to any slowdown that accompanies the coronavirus. Slow or fast, the virus will spread.[29] At the current rate of contagion, it appears that the spread is occurring relatively quickly, at least in terms of span of geography.[30]

Widespread disruption is on the horizon.[31] We have already seen Apple's supply chains disrupted.[32] Difficulties are mounting in China. Our coming to terms with the nature of this spread is leading many to panic. Unfortunately, during a panic, our cognitive capacities may not do the best job of integrating all pertinent facts into decision making.

This problem seems to hold for those formulating monetary policy at present. I will review macroeconomic and financial markets through the lens of supply and demand to the elaborate mechanics of disruption and the relevant options for monetary policy.

---

29 Hanson, Robin. 2020. "Deliberate Exposure Intuition." *OvercomingBias*, February 17.

30 Worldometer. 2020. "Coronavirus Cases." *Worldometer*.

31 Schneider, Grace. 2020. "UPS says coronavirus is already cutting demand and disrupting supply chains." *MSN.com*, March 11.

32 Stankiewicz, Kevin. 2020. "Cramer says Apple's stock may not be done falling in coronavirus-driven plunge." *CNBC*, February 28.

MONETARY POLICY IS NOT SUITED TO OFFSET NEGATIVE AGGREGATE SUPPLY SHOCKS

As a general rule, the Fed should not attempt to remedy a negative aggregate supply shock with monetary policy. Monetary policy is useful in offsetting slowdowns that occur due to negative aggregate demand shocks. Falls in the value of total expenditures that occur due to either an increase in demand to hold money or a decrease in the quantity of money lead to temporary macroeconomic disruption. The value of total expenditures fails to match the total value of goods expected to be sold across a given period. Either a fall in the average level of prices or an increase in the quantity of money can offset this discrepancy.

The case is different for an autonomous fall in aggregate supply. A negative supply shock entails a fall in the level of output that can be supported by a given capital structure. This may occur, as in the present case, due to prolonged disruption of supply chains. Currently, the volume of trade is falling and is likely to continue falling as nations take precautions to slow the spread of the coronavirus.

All else equal, any fall in real GDP that we experience will be a textbook real business cycle, with the aggregate supply curve shifting left. The fall in the availability of goods will lead to a general increase in prices. Since expectations seem to be moving quickly, prices may move ahead of the fall in supply as individuals rush to the store to stock up on goods. An increase in the quantity of money would only exacerbate this problem.

Conversely, attempts to offset any increase in inflation due to the fall in income would only lead to further detriment. To maintain a 2 percent rate of inflation in the face of a negative aggregate supply shock, the Federal Reserve would have to slow the rate of growth of the stock of base money in circulation. This is a fundamental problem with price level and inflation targeting.

To maintain a constant rate of inflation, a negative aggregate supply shock must be offset by a reduction in aggregate demand. I doubt this will be the policy of choice, but mindless pursuit of the 2 percent inflation target could lead to such an outcome. It is unclear what policy makers will view as the optimal path for monetary policy.

SAYING ONE THING AND MEANING ANOTHER

There also are difficulties in interpreting financial conditions and identifying distortions created by Federal Reserve intervention in short-term lending markets. The situation is more complicated in financial markets. A negative aggregate supply shock could lead to a negative aggregate demand shock if the fall in business activity degrades the solvency of borrowers, leaving many unable to repay loans or acquire revolving credit lines on which their businesses typically depend. *Or*, reflecting changes in underlying conditions, demand for credit at existing rates may fall as trade slows.

In this case, falling rates are a symptom of falling demand for credit in light of lower growth. Credit supply constraints are causing difficulties for business in places affected by the coronavirus.[33] An increase in such difficulties could impact capital structure for years to come, so it is not clear we can discount the significance of this interpretation. In either case, it is difficulties arising in financial markets that are likely behind Powell's forward guidance promising potential

---

33 BBC News. 2020. "Coronavirus credit crunch hits millions of Chinese firms." *BBC News*, February 24.

support from the Federal Reserve.[34] Fed officials would like to avoid structural damage from an epidemic.

But what is the nature of support from the Federal Reserve? The apparent intervention by the Federal Reserve is actually alleviating the difficulties created by its own policy.

Let's suppose that the current fall in rates represents a rational response to a fall in profitable investment opportunities. In that case, *lowering the federal funds rate target would not represent artificial support, but equilibration.* What is preventing credit markets from reaching equilibrium? The rate paid on excess reserves is acting as a price floor. If I am correct, the yield curve inversion is an artifact of Federal Reserve intervention in short-term lending markets.

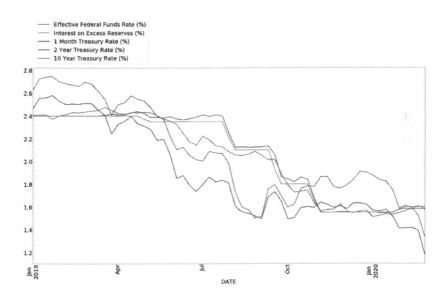

---

34 Rugaber, Christopher. 2020. "Fed chair Jerome Powell: Will 'use our tools' to support economy." *The Washington Times*, February 28.

Short-term rates likely would also fall, except that the rate paid on excess reserves sets a price floor that can only be adjusted by Federal Reserve policy. The rate paid on excess reserves is the relevant alternative to holding short-term financial instruments. Thus, the effective federal funds rate hovers around the true risk-free rate: the rate paid on excess reserves. In the face of economic decline, long-term rates are falling while short-term rates remain elevated.

A decade ago, I might have characterized this as a rush to liquidity. But this does not appear to be the case with the current yield curve inversion. Long-term rates have fallen below short-term rates on expectation of a negative aggregate supply shock.

For Powell to lower the federal funds rate target and the rate paid on excess reserves would not artificially stimulate investment but, rather, prevent the rate paid on excess reserves from acting as an interest rate floor. As with any effective price control, when conditions governing supply and demand schedules change, that price control can exert a disequilibrating effect.

CONCLUSION

The nature of monetary conditions may not be clear, but two facts are. First, the Federal Reserve should *not* respond to a negative aggregate supply shock by boosting aggregate demand. However, if the situation devolves into a credit crisis, then the standard tools used to stabilize aggregate demand might be appropriate. Second, the interest rate paid on excess reserves is acting as an interest rate floor and is likely playing a significant role in the current yield curve inversion.

A lowering of the federal funds target, in this case, would allow credit markets to generate a mix of investments that would predominate absent monetary intervention.

The Federal Reserve is likely trying to balance its support for federal borrowing with this current supply-side disruption. The true difficulty lies in balancing these emerging difficulties with the responsibility for federal borrowing which the Federal Reserve has assumed in the last decade.

ANTI-GOUGING LAWS CAN KILL
BY RAYMOND C. NILES

March 3, 2020.

Much has been made in the media about the Surgeon General's recent Twitter exhortation, "Seriously people – STOP BUYING MASKS! They are NOT effective in preventing general [sic] public from catching Coronavirus."[35]

But what is usually left out is the rest of his tweet, "…but if healthcare providers can't get them to care for sick patients, it puts them and our communities at risk!"

I am not a medical doctor, so I have no particular expertise in evaluating whether masks help prevent infection in the general public. Although I do find it interesting that masks are recommended for those *caring* for infected people, so masks apparently are effective at preventing infection, if used properly (and a big deal is made about how difficult it is to properly "fit" the mask over one's face—just how hard can that be??).

But I am an economist, so I find the under-reported second part of his tweet very interesting and revealing. Is the Surgeon General advising people not to buy masks because they are not helpful in preventing infection, or is he advising people not to buy masks because he is worried about a shortage, and wants to ensure that the existing

---

35 U.S. Surgeon General. 2020. "Seriously people- STOP BUYING MASKS! They are NOT effective in preventing general public from catching #Coronavirus, but if healthcare providers can't get them to care for sick patients, it puts them and our communities at risk!" *Twitter*, February 29. https://twitter.com/Surgeon_General/status/1233725785283932160.

supply of masks be available for those who most crucially need it: the doctors and nurses and loved ones who are caring for sick patients?

I wish the Surgeon General had studied economics. The Law of Supply and Demand—the most fundamental principle of economics—tells us that shortages cannot exist when prices are allowed to adjust to changes in supply and demand. Or, to put it another way, shortages *only* arise when the price mechanism is impeded, whether by law or by custom.

In the United States, and around the world, both law and custom prevent market prices from adjusting when such adjustment is most urgently needed: when there is a supply disruption and/or a spike in demand for that product. That is happening right now, when it comes to "N95" masks, the type that filter out 95% of particles and are deemed most effective in preventing the spread of coronavirus.

I actually bought a box of 10 of these masks last year for a trip to Mumbai, India, where I used them—quite successfully—to protect me from the highly polluted air in that city. It cost about $15. Yet today at all of the drug and hardware stores around town that used to sell these masks, I see signs on their front doors that say, "No masks available."

Demand has spiked for these masks. This spike in demand, whether it is based on sound medical opinion or not, is a fact. If prices were allowed to adjust, they would rise. This would have two effects. First, it would reduce the quantity purchased. Those who were not willing to pay the higher price for the masks would not get them, while those who urgently needed the masks—and could pay for them (think: hospitals!)—would find them readily available.

Economists often describe this salutary "rationing" effect of higher prices. It means that those who most urgently want and need the masks, and can pay for them, will get them, while those who value them less will not get the masks.

However, the higher prices have an even greater salutary effect on the supply side. It is greater and longer-term, because the higher prices induce an increase in the *production* of masks. Higher prices signal higher profits to be made in making the masks. This means that factories can afford to bring on extra shifts, hire more trucks, pay more for scarce supplies—do all that it takes to make more masks to meet the extra demand.

The result—if market prices are allowed to adjust—is that while the quantities demanded are temporarily curtailed to meet the available supply, the quantities supplied begin to radically increase. The result is that more masks become available, and prices eventually fall. Eventually, they will fall to nearly the "typical" or "normal" level that preceded the outbreak of coronavirus, but with shelves full of masks. No shortages!

But instead of finding (temporarily expensive) masks available for sale, we are confronted by "No masks available" signs everywhere we look.

We have caused this potentially deadly shortage of masks with our antipathy to "price gouging." That antipathy is deeply embedded in our culture. We decry "price gougers" at sporting events, or who sell drugs at "unconscionably high" prices or who simply charge prices that we do not like!

This cultural antipathy to high prices has found its way into laws. In the past 25 years, some 34 states have passed laws that prohibit "price gouging."[36] It is defined in various ways, some more objectively than others. In California, it is illegal to raise the price of a product

---

36 Giberson, Michael. 2012. "Thirty-four states and the District of Columbia have anti-price gouging laws." *Knowledge Problem*, November 3.

during an emergency by more than 10% from what it was before the emergency. In Florida, the law simply says that it is illegal to charge an "unconscionably high" price for an "essential commodity" during an "emergency."[37] Good luck defining those terms.

The result is that the CEOs of businesses, such as CVS Drug or TrueValue Hardware, perhaps just to avoid the wrath of their customers who hate price gouging, or to comply with the anti-gouging laws, whether vaguely worded or not, simply choose not to raise prices of goods during an emergency.

Instead, they simply let their supplies run out. They cannot increase their orders because they cannot pay more for the goods to their wholesalers who, in turn, cannot pay more to the manufacturer who, in turn, is unable to call in the extra shifts, pay the overtime, rush in the urgently needed supplies, etc., to make more of the masks...

Or the generators, or the gasoline...

In 2006, in a notorious case, a man who wanted to bring in generators from out of state during Hurricane Katrina was jailed, and his generators confiscated, while the governor of Mississippi, Sonny Perdue, proclaimed that he would step up enforcement action against price gougers.[38]

In Florida, gas station owners preferred to let their gasoline run out rather than charge more money for gasoline, which would have incentivized gasoline wholesalers (at greater cost to themselves) to ship in urgently needed gas from other parts of the country that were

---

37 2011. "Regulation of Trade, Commerce, Investment, and Solicitations Chapter 501 Consumer Protection." *MyFloridaLegal*.

38 Stossel, John & Gena Binkley. 2006. "MYTH: Price-Gouging Is Bad." *ABC News*, May 17.

not devastated by the hurricane.[39]

Generators, gasoline and (probably) face masks are urgently needed during disasters and emergencies, such as hurricanes or outbreaks of new viruses.

And the only way we can ensure their ready supply is to allow prices to rise.

It is time that Americans—and everyone around the world— embrace price gouging and recognize it as the vital and life-saving market mechanism that ensures that supplies reach their most urgent, life-saving uses, and that more of these supplies are manufactured and distributed.

A first step is to repeal the silly and non-objective "price gouging" laws on the books of 34 states. A second, more fundamental step is to understand the economics of supply and demand. It is high time that all of us abandon the term "price gouging" and call it what it is: supply and demand. And recognize the life-saving value of unimpeded market prices, whether those prices are "high" or not.

I have just one of those N95 masks left and see lots of "No masks available" signs at the stores that used to sell them around me. I hope I don't get coronavirus.

---

39 Mouawad, Jad & Simon Romero. 2005. "Gas Prices Surge as Supply Drops." *The New York Times*, September 1.

SHOULD GOVERNMENT GO MEDIEVAL DURING PANDEMIC DISEASE?
BY ROBERT E. WRIGHT

March 4, 2020.

Americans are only now becoming aware that government claims sweeping powers in the case of pandemic disease. An order can be given by the U.S. president. Your house, block, town, or city can be quarantined without notice. You could find yourself trapped. You can be forced into a sick camp. Non-compliance is enforced with criminal penalties.

This might sound alarming to you but many pundits are on board with using such medieval tactics.

Donald G. McNeil Jr., a reasonable-sounding reporter for *The New York Times*, has written the following:[40]

> Close the borders, quarantine the ships, pen terrified citizens up inside their poisoned cities. For the first time in more than a century, the world has chosen to confront a new and terrifying virus with the iron fist instead of the latex glove. At least for a while, it worked, and it might still serve a purpose.

He frankly favors, in his words, "choosing brutality over freedom." Many people would no doubt agree.

And yet, human beings have a natural right to self-preservation. They exist for their own enjoyment, not to serve as the pawns of anyone

---

40 McNeil, Donald G. Jr. 2020. "To Take On the Coronavirus, Go Medieval on It." *The New York Times*, February 28.

or anything, even during putative crises.

Like the rest of the U.S. Constitution, the Bill of Rights does not explicitly protect the right of individual Americans to breathe the air, drink potable water, expel bodily waste products, or do countless other things necessary to live. That was not a massive oversight on the part of the Founders; it reflected their view that the purpose of government was to protect the natural human rights triad of life, liberty, and property. Any law or policy that endangered the triad was not just unconstitutional but anathema to natural human rights.

While government might limit riparian rights or where individuals may lawfully urinate and defecate (and green taxes on flatulence seem well nigh inevitable), no government committed to the well-being of its citizenry would dare to overburden basic biological functions because to do so would be an obvious repudiation of the government's prime directive to protect, rather than limit or take, life, liberty, and property.

The Founders envisaged government's protective role as a limited, not a paternal, one. In particular, government should not dictate how individuals manage any trade-offs within the natural human rights triad. Some may prefer dear life over all else, but others may prefer liberty (e.g., give me liberty or give me death) or property over life (e.g., DNRO), and their preferences may change over time and context.[41]

Government should take available, effective steps to prevent people from spreading disease, shooting, or otherwise harming others, but it should not dictate what people must, or can't, do to protect their own lives.

---

41 Henry, Patrick. 1775. "Give Me Liberty Or Give Me Death." *Yale Law School*, The Avalon Project. "What is a DNR (DNRO)? | Free DNR Form Florida." *Elder Needs Law*, November 14.

For example, it might stop an American from entering the U.S. from Wuhan or some other COVID-19 hotspot, but it should not prevent Americans from going to one of those places if they so choose. It can remonstrate, inform, and warn of re-entry restrictions but it should not stop people from making their own choices, even if death is certain, and it certainly shouldn't restrict liberty when sickness or death remains improbable.

Many government attempts to protect individuals seem impressive at first but ultimately pale compared to individual precautions. Food safety, for example, relies more on individual judgements and private inspection than the public apparatus.[42]

The same goes for drug use. Government should prevent Americans from harming others to the extent possible but it should not limit liberty because some people abuse drugs and end up driving while impaired or robbing a convenience store. The latter are crimes but criminalizing drug use simply because it might increase other crimes is unwarranted and, as we have learned time and again, unwise.

Bearing arms presents a parallel example. Government should prevent gun violence to the extent possible but it should not limit the liberty of all because a few people (and it is a small percentage of gun owners, especially outside of the drug trade context) shoot innocents, even themselves or loved ones.

Some states, like my beloved California and New Jersey, restrict

---

42 Wright, Robert E. 2019. "Unsung Heroes: Private Food Inspectors." *American Institute for Economic Research*, December 29.

the bearing of arms.[43] But then should it not follow that if defenseless Mary is raped, Gary robbed, and poor Granny killed, the state should be held liable? After all, states with stringent handgun laws are essentially saying, "We don't trust you to protect yourself, so we will do it for you," though, all too often, they do not.

Of course states have no resources of their own and could simply raise taxes to pay for their failures. If payments to victims came out of the personal estates of the policymakers who supported gun control legislation, though, legislative paternalism would quickly fade as they would have some proverbial skin in the game. Ditto if policymakers overstep while attempting to stop a pandemic after it has become unstoppable.[44]

Some people may concede the general point but then add, "But surely we do not want people to own cannon or anti-aircraft missiles or nukes, so where do you draw the line?" Incentives reduce such perceived problems. Few individuals who could afford a nuclear bomb would have an incentive to use it and those with sufficient incentive to do so would not be deterred by a law. (Or economic sanctions apparently.)

Moreover, unrestricted ownership of anti-aircraft weapons would have ameliorated, if not outright prevented, the 9-11 attacks because surely some corporation, or a consortium of them (probably led by an insurance company), would have provided effective cover for lower

43 Wright, Robert E. 2020. "How to Save California From Itself." *American Institute for Economic Research*, February 24; Wright, Robert E. 2019. "Wage Floors Are Making My Son a Delinquent." *American Institute for Economic Research*, July 19.

44 Caton, James L. "The Coronavirus Reveals the Limits of Monetary Policy." *American Institute for Economic Research*, March 2.

Manhattan and other vulnerable private assets. Knowing that, the terrorists would not have even tried and we could still wear our shoes through airport security lines.

If ending restrictions on the types of weapons citizens can own sounds extreme, recall that for- and non-profit corporations have a long history of owning military-grade ordnance. Private military forces equipped with cannon played pivotal roles in the Revolution and War of 1812 as privateers (legal pirates basically), legionnaires, and private militia "companies."

But, critics wail, we have "state capacity" now. Do we really, though? I see a horrifically expensive military well-equipped and trained to defeat traditional military foes but incapable of quelling determined resistance forces even if given decades and trillions of dollars to do so.[45] I also see lots of paramilitary police forces that can quell riots but can't protect momma or pop pop on the street because nobody in the neighborhood trusts police officers to do the right thing.

The modern state is quite "capable" when it comes raising revenue but even there it remains highly inefficient, taxing many things that should not be taxed and doing so in many awkward ways instead of taxing a few items sensibly, as Adam Smith and Alexander Hamilton admonished.

So where some see state capacity, I see mostly incapacity. Government can influence events, but usually only by making matters worse. It seems poised to do so again with its response to COVID-19.

It is high time that Americans stop pretending the government can protect everyone, in every possible way, all the time and tell

45 Hartung, William D. 2020. "Trump Is Trying to Ride the Pentagon Gravy Train to Reelection." *Mises Institute*, Mises Wire, March 2.

Washington to stop overstepping. Americans are not children and bureaucrats are not parents, not even bad ones; they are people with more power, especially during ostensible public health emergencies, than the Founders intended even POTUS to possess.

So, no, we should not go medieval on COVID-19. We should still embrace freedom.

THE INSOLUBLE PERILS OF PREDICTION
BY JOAKIM BOOK

March 14, 2020.

Predictions have always been fraught with perils.[46] Gauging the future is tricky business, a business filled with well-meaning and serious commentators drowned out by pranksters and ideologically committed imbeciles. Despite being wholly unequipped for the task of divining the future, most political pundits and financial commentators are revered as saints for their extraordinary abilities to misjudge the future.

We ought to treat most predictions with a large chunk of skepticism. We should reject vaguely phrased and imprecise ones, not because they couldn't carry some valuable insight, but because they cannot be assessed.

If I forecast a future recession, but not what will cause it or trigger it, how long it will last, how bad it will be, and where it will strike, I'm not making much of a prediction; I'm not providing any information beyond extrapolating the known past. Recessions, like earthquakes and shark attacks, occasionally happen, and saying that they will happen again is trivial and does not mean others ought to admire me for my fantastic foresight.

Statistically, too, there are usually only a handful of ways that a prediction can come true—but a myriad, even infinite, ways that it can go wrong. If all these possible scenarios are equally likely (which they of course aren't), we should almost never expect a particular

---

46 Book, Joakim. 2019. "What Does It Mean to Have Predicted an Economic Event?" *American Institute for Economic Research*, February 22.

prediction to hold true.[47]

The challenge is, as popular economist Tim Harford stated before interviewing Philip Tetlock, author of the celebrated *Superforcasting: The Art and Science of Prediction*: in a myriad of predictions of varying quality, how do you find the Cassandras amidst the Chicken Littles?[48]

Well, let's track them, said Tetlock after noting that political "experts" were repeatedly asked for their conjectures even after having seen their previous prediction gone entirely wrong. Let's see how often they are right. For decades, Tetlock has run this research program, measuring the forecasters' success at predicting things.[49]

In regards to environmentalists' outrageous claims about the future, Toby Young at the *Spectator* said refreshingly that rather than get demoralized about misinformation and hyperbole, "we should be grateful that these gloomsters make such oddly precise predictions."[50] That lets us measure the predictions, assess them, and subsequently discard the gloomsters' opinions when enough of their predictions have gone the opposite way: "It's like putting a sell-by date on their credibility," rejoices Young.

From global famines in the 1970s to the hilarious projection that

47 Book, Joakim. 2019. "The Paradox of Prediction." *Notes on Liberty*, February 20.

48 2020. "Tim Harford on Persuasion and Popular Economics (Ep. 87)." *Conversations with Tyler*, February 12; BBC. 2020. "More or Less: Superforecasting, wood burning stoves and the real story of Hidden Figures." *BBC Radio*, February 28; Tetlock, Philip E. & Dan Gardner. 2015. *Superforecasting: The Art and Science of Prediction*. Broadway Books.

49 Wikipedia. 2020. "The Good Judgment Project." *Wikipedia*, February 16.

50 Young, Toby. 2020. "Climate doomsayers keep putting sell-by dates on their credibility." *Spectator USA*, January 30.

Spain by 2020 will be uninhabitably hot and ridden with malaria, to cataclysmic sea-level rises and mass extinctions and climate change deaths in our century, environmental doomsday prophets have made this into a sport that we should delight in playing.[51]

Let me play prediction follow-up with another gloomster, the NYU economics professor Nouriel Roubini, known in the financial press as Dr. Doom for having predicted the housing crash in 2007—or, more precisely, having called doom-and-gloom enough times to accidentally be vindicated by future events.[52]

IRAN, OIL PRICES, AND THE BLACK CORONAVIRUS SWAN

In January, Dr. Roubini gave a series of talks at the Norwegian asset-management company Skagen's prestigious annual conference.[53] At the time, his lecture seemed very thoughtful and nicely put together. To remind you of the incessant noise that is global news, in the background were escalating conflicts with Iran, worry about the impacts of oil prices on a frail economy, and U.S. trade wars.

True to his reputation, Roubini painted a dire macro picture of the

51 Williams, Thomas D. 2020. "Remembering Climate Alarmists' False Prophecies." *Breitbart*, February 12; Wilson, Jamie. 1999. "Tourist spots could be too hot to handle." *The Guardian*, August 29; Lomborg, Bjørn. 2019. "Humans Can Survive Underwater." *Project Syndicate*, November 21; Brand, Stewart. 2015. "Rethinking extinction." *Aeon*, April 21; Lewis, Marlo Jr. 2019. "Climate-Related Deaths Are at Historic Lows, Data Show." *Foundation for Economic Education*, June 7; Shellenberger, Michael. 2019. "Why Apocalyptic Claims About Climate Change Are Wrong." *Forbes*, November 25.

52 "Faculty: Nouriel Roubini." *NYU Stern School of Business*; Book, Joakim. 2019. "What's the Difference Between Michael Burry and Alexander Fordyce?" *American Institute for Economic Research*, November 13.

53 Skagen. 2020. "Nyårskonferensen." *Skagen*.

new decade: Purchasing Managers' Index data and other forward-looking indicators for the major economies kept coming in lukewarm at best.[54] The trade deal with China that we have now all but forgotten about looked bleak. Hovering in the background was Brexit, with its many possible and dire outcomes, and in January the telenovela that is the presidential election seemed like it could go in absolutely any direction.

Roubini very neatly tied together three different topics and how they were likely to impact each other: Iran, oil prices, and global growth. It was a plausible story: oil prices matter for global growth as oil is the master industry that powers every other industry, and what happens politically and militarily with Iran can certainly move oil prices a lot.[55]

Here's my stylized summary of Roubini's argument:

Scenario	Global Growth	Iran-U.S. Conflict	Oil Prices	Roubini's likelihood
1	Expansion (3.4%)	Return to normal	Below $70	5%
2	Slowdown (3.0%)	Military escalation	$70-80	45%

54 Roubini, Nouriel. "Outlook for the Global Economy, Oil Prices, Macro Policies and Markets: Investors Severely Underpricing The Risks of a US-Iran Escalation and Conflict." *Skagen Conference*, presentation slides.

55 Epstein, Alex. 2019. "The New Moral Case for Fossil Fuels." *Capitalism Magazine*, October 8.

3	Further Slowdown (2.7%)	Direct Military Exchange	$80-100	30%
4	Global Recession (<2.5%)	Full-scale war	>$100	20%

At the time the projections were sound and serious; these were the issues of the day. Yes, his causal mechanism and assessment of Iran's political options seemed sensible. Perhaps we could quibble over the exact estimates—were we really facing a one-in-five chance of *full-scale war* with Iran?—but overall, it was a perfectly reasonable story.

Enter reality. coronavirus scare, pandemic chaos, draconian government actions, and an outbreak in Iran that wholly re-arranged everyone's priorities.[56] In Iran, as in most countries, the focus of politics swiftly changed to epidemics, health care, and travel restrictions rather than political grandstanding over energy, influence, or oil. Governments left and right went bananas, enforcing one centrally planned authoritarian restriction after another.[57]

Enter reality round two: the Saudi Arabia–Russia oil price war meant that global oil prices fell rapidly and massively when the Saudis ordered large increases of production—oil producers are "flooding the market simultaneously in a game of chicken," wrote *The Wall Street*

---

56 Tamny, John. 2020. "Economic Crisis Is the State's Oxygen." *American Institute for Economic Research*, March 9.

57 See article herein entitled "They Are Rewriting the History of Coronavirus in Real Time."; See article herein entitled "The Free Market Provides What We Need to Survive a Pandemic."

Journal's Spencer Jakab.[58]

While the news is still fresh and the precise reasons are not yet known, efforts seem to have been aimed at squeezing Russian and American oil producers in order to improve its own market share. The move from $55 per barrel, where crude had been trading during February ($58 when Roubini spoke on January 17) to below $30 in intra-day trading on Monday made Roubini's prediction about oil prices entirely obsolete.

Prices of less than half of Roubini's lowest (and least likely) scenario were associated with U.S-Iran peace and a thriving world economy. Instead we're looking at a paralyzed Iran with upwards of 10,000 people infected, a country too busy with its medical emergency to heed the prediction of some gloomy economics professor; we're not looking at war with Iran, but global production at a standstill, ruthless travel and commercial restrictions in many countries, and a possible global recession.[59]

Not that it prevented Roubini from publicly claiming that he predicted this and that the coronavirus outbreak and oil shocks are "a true signal

58 Earle, Peter C. 2020. "Don't Sweat the Crash in Oil Prices." *American Institute for Economic Research*, March 10; Faucon, Benoit & Summer Said. 2020. "Saudis Instigate Oil-Price Clash With Russia." *The Wall Street Journal*, March 8; Jakab, Spencer. 2020. "OPEC, R.I.P." *The Wall Street Journal*, March 8.

59 Roser, Max, Hannah Ritchie, Esteban Ortiz-Ospina. "Coronavirus Disease (COVID-19) – Statistics and Research." Our World in Data, March 19; CDC. 2020. "Cases in U.S." Centers for Disease Control and Prevention, March 19.

of upcoming global recession."[60] I thought war with Iran and rapidly *increasing* oil prices were his main risk factors for global recession...?

We can invoke the black swan, Nassim Taleb's almost tired analogy for sudden and unexpected tail-risk events.[61] Just a few weeks ago, Roubini's careful analysis seemed prudent and probable. Then the world happened, and his impressive predictions were worth nothing.

Naturally, it is too much to expect Dr. Roubini to have foreseen the impact and domino effect of this pandemic. The point here isn't that things can't change and that predictions made on outdated information must hold, but how shaky forecasts are in the face of market reality, human psychology, politics, and black swans.

Stuff happens, and your carefully laid plans and sensibly argued projections are quickly overthrown.

The lesson here is twofold: the reality of our world includes sudden events that cause all kinds of unforeseen turmoil. And puffed-up sooth-sayers, however lucky their forecasts might have been in the past, are usually completely wrong. When some of them are right, as the law of large numbers and the existence of overconfident know-it-alls guarantee, we should probably not credit them too much.

Lottery winners are, after all, not impressively divining seers.

---

60 Mohamed, Theron. 2020. "Coronavirus will send stocks and oil into 'free fall' and shrink the global economy, 'Dr. Doom' economist warns." *Markets Insider*, March 9; Nouriel Roubini. 2020. "The week will start with US and global equities down another 2-3%, credit spreads blowing up especially for HY & credit markets seized and frozen, 10 year Treas yields even lower, & oil prices sharply down." *Twitter*, tweet from March 8. https://twitter.com/Nouriel/status/1236780797438373888.

61 Wikipedia. 2020. "The Black Swan: The Impact of the Highly Improbable." *Wikipedia*, March 12.

COVID-19 PROMPTS THE QUESTION: WHY VALUE HUMAN LIFE?
BY JEFFREY TUCKER

March 7, 2020.

Have you noticed how philosophical COVID-19 is making us? The possible presence of imminent death of so many—true or not—is causing a reassessment of fundamental issues.

I'm not just talking about the issue of which groceries we should stockpile. The answer to that question based on what I observed at Costco last week is apparent: toilet paper.

People are also asking big questions. Like: why value freedom? Like: why value human life?

For example, in private conversation, a friend of mine offered an interesting view of COVID-19. He said, look, why actually should we care when people die in large numbers from disease? Maybe this is nature's way of culling the population of less healthy people. Happens in the animal kingdom all the time. Why get all emotional and freaked out about this?

He was very serious. I'm guessing you have heard some version of the same.

Before you dismiss the observation entirely as ghastly and cruel, I can promise you that this view is oddly common among people who have read just enough Darwin to get the main point, particularly his expressed regrets about life-saving medical advances (it was just a tossed-off observation he had that went very wrong).

In 1871, Darwin wrote as follows:

There is reason to believe that vaccination has preserved thousands, who from a weak constitution would formerly have succumbed to small-pox. Thus the weak members of civilised societies propagate their kind. No one who has attended to the breeding of domestic animals will doubt that this must be highly injurious to the race of man. It is surprising how soon a want of care, or care wrongly directed, leads to the degeneration of a domestic race; but excepting in the case of man himself, hardly any one is so ignorant as to allow his worst animals to breed...

The observation that prolonging longer than a state of nature would allow is "injurious" would pertain to anything that lifted up the human population, such as the wide availability of housing, food, medicine, and sanitation. Weird, right?

However, he then continued:

but if we were intentionally to neglect the weak and helpless, it could only be for a contingent benefit, with an overwhelming present evil. Hence we must bear without complaining the undoubtedly bad effects of the weak surviving and propagating their kind; but there appears to be at least one check in steady action, namely the weaker and inferior members of society not marrying so freely as the sound; and this check might be indefinitely increased, though this is more to be hoped for than expected...

Better that he finds mass death evil but it's still weird that he finds some evolutionary "benefit" in letting the weak die, and hoped for some way to keep inferiors from propagating. There is every reason to believe that this passage helped encourage the rise of eugenic theory that led to mass sterilizations, segregations, economic regulations, zoning, and, later, grim experiments in population control and worse. The demographic panics of the late 19th century, and the resulting belief that human dignity is contingent and life expendable for larger aims, culminated in the 20th century's wars, death camps, purges, famines, and mass murder by the state.

Even today, you can find people who regret the flourishing of humans with their incessant and chaotic breeding patterns. Extremists on the right can't shake the sense that the wrong people are multiplying their kind while the right people are failing to breed enough—as if only ideology knows the best mix that is right for the world. Extremists on the left, meanwhile, are prone to believe that human life and industrial capitalism that has led to mass population increases are something to regret and control if not entirely tamp down. And this is one reason there is so much confirmation bias on the left with climate-change frenzies.

So let us return to basics: why should we defend human life and commit resources to preserving and prolonging it? Why cure disease rather than allow those weak enough to succumb to bite the dust so the strong can inherit the earth?

The answer is as follows. The great contribution of Enlightenment thinking was to settle on the idea of the value of human life and the belief that it should be protected and that all people should flourish in freedom and prosperity when possible. Human energies should be put to making human life better for as many people as possible. People have rights, and deserve to be treated with dignity. All people.

This is a modern view—perhaps taken over from Christianity's early years (St. Augustine was passionate on this point on grounds that the human person is made in God's image) but realized most fully after the rise of prosperity in the late Middle Ages.[62] It became obvious for the first time that wealth could grow, that classes could be fluid, that life could be extended, that the population could grow and grow, that we could progress together. With that evidence came the entrenchment of a commitment to individual rights and a longing for universal emancipation and the good life for all.

A related commitment emerged to the cause of medical science not just to help the few but to improve the whole lot of humanity. That sounds like a great idea but not if we live in a zero-sum world in which your riches come at my expense or your good emerges only as a result of the harm imposed by others. But when it became clear—as Enlightenment theory had it—that there is no inherent conflict between the good of one and the good of many, a new moral imperative swept the world. The idea of "do unto others" became thoroughly operational in practice. "Act so that you treat humanity, whether in your own person or in that of another, always as an end and never as a means only," said Immanuel Kant.

Over time, it became widely believed that to value and protect life from invasion by external forces is a core principle of civilization. This became the philosophical presumption on which modernity itself was built. Freedom was a corollary for both moral and practical reasons. Freedom works to build wealth for one and all; it was also the right thing to do to unleash as much human energy as possible in the quest for a better world.

Economic science became the handmaiden of this idea of universal

---

62 2019. Section 6.2 'The Human Mind as an Image of God' in "Saint Augustine." *Stanford Encyclopedia of Philosophy*, September 25.

rights for two reasons. First, economics explained precisely how it is that wealth can expand from the privileged few to the whole of society, such that we don't have to steal to get a bit to eat and kill to live a long life. Second, economics innovated the concept of the "division of labor" which showed scientifically how everyone benefits from the cooperative work and creativity of everyone else. The "weak" are just as valuable to the building of human community as the "strong."

This is why Adam Smith's glorious two books—*The Wealth of Nations* and *The Theory of Moral Sentiments*—are such high contributions to human knowledge. They gave humanity the best reason ever to value itself and protect itself from any and all dangers. If one person suffers unnecessarily, we all are diminished. If we can use intelligence, creativity, and resources to aid anyone in need, we all benefit.

This is a philosophical proposition that turned to a moral commitment. It was this foundational belief that gave rise to the good life we live today, with long lives, universal access to amazing technology, food and health for all, and the daily struggle to improve life on earth without limit. We all benefit from this conviction, every day.

I dare say that many of us today are only alive because of this philosophical proposition. I know for sure this is true in my case.

This is why we should care.

The issue that deserves serious debate right now is not whether life is worth saving but the best means of doing so and at what cost to the whole. For reasons that are unclear, COVID-19 has inspired officials around the world to pursue a strategy of containment, along with draconian quarantines and forcible controls on movement, rather than the more conventional route of disease mitigation, as with every other disease.

Holman Jenkins sums up the problem nicely: "At what point

should we stop working so hard to prevent transmission to people who most likely will have a mild flu- or cold-like experience in hopes of preventing a small percentage of severe cases that require costly medical intervention?"[63]

That's a serious question.

As for the big picture, no, humanity does not need a good old-fashioned plague every once in a while. We need ever better means of curing the sick, feeding the hungry, housing the homeless, prolonging the lives of the aged, and generally caring for the least among us, and we should do this in our own interest lest we too fall victim to the plight of the least fortunate.

63 Jenkins, Holman W. Jr. 2020. "A Chinese Mystery and Covid-19's Economic Puzzle." *The Wall Street Journal*, March 6.

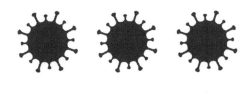

THE CRISIS
HITS

WHY THIS DRACONIAN RESPONSE TO COVID-19?
BY JEFFREY TUCKER

March 8, 2020.

Imagine if you are the organizer of a major arts and tech event that attracts a quarter-million attendees. One week out from the conference, the mayor cancels your event. Your event is not named specifically, just that all events involving more than 2,500 people are officially banned. He does this using emergency powers, justified in the name of containing a virus.

And that's it. This is what happened to South by Southwest, one of the most important events in the world in Austin, Texas, which has thus far not reported a single case of COVID-19. Based on last year's numbers, It's the end for:

- 73,716 conference attendees and 232,258 festival attendees; 4,700 speakers
- 4,331 media/press attendees
- 2,124 sessions
- 70,000 trade show attendees occupying 181,400 square feet of exhibit space
- 351 official parties and events
- 612 international acts
- 1,964 performance acts

Local merchants are devastated. All hotel and flight reservations are lost. Countless contracts have been voided by executive fiat. It's a financial calamity for the city (last year brought half a billion dollars for local merchants) and for untold millions of people affected by the abrupt decision.

Draconian, to say the least.

Making matters worse, a vicious and completely false report published by *Variety* said that the festival was aching for the city to make the call so that the festival could collect insurance money.[64] This turns out to be entirely wrong: South by Southwest had no insurance against infectious disease.[65] It was a smear and response to mass frenzy. After all, a petition on Change.org signed by 55,000 people had demanded the cancellation.

The city acquiesced to the mob. A grand and glorious conference was destroyed—the first of many this season.

Italy now has 16 million people under quarantine, which is to say that they are prisoners.[66]

> Anyone living in Lombardy and 14 other central and northern provinces will need special permission to travel. Milan and Venice are both affected. Prime Minister Giuseppe Conte also announced the closure of schools, gyms, museums, nightclubs and other venues across the whole country. The measures, the most radical taken outside China, will last until 3 April.

---

64 Willman, Chris. 2020. "Why Isn't SXSW Canceled Yet? It May Come Down to Insurance and the City." *Variety*, March 5.

65 Haring, Bruce. 2020. "SXSW Founders: No Coverage For Disease Cancellation In Our Event Insurance Policies." *Deadline*, March 6.

66 BBC News. 2020. "Coronavirus: Northern Italy quarantines 16 million people." *BBC News*, March 8.

Americans have been quarantined on cruise ships and then forced to pay for their later hospitalization.[67] The government that quarantines you has zero intention to pay the costs associated with your care, to say nothing of the opportunity costs of missing work.

The press isn't helping. *The New York Times* has cheered it all on, aggressively advocating that governments go medieval on this one.[68]

In six months, if we are in a recession, unemployment is up, financial markets are wrecked, and people are locked in their homes, we'll wonder why the heck governments chose disease "containment" over disease mitigation. Then the conspiracy theorists get to work.

The containment strategy was never debated or discussed. For the first time in modern history, governments of the world have taken it upon themselves to control population flows in the hopes of stemming the spread of this disease—regardless of the cost and with scant evidence that this strategy will actually work.

More and more, the containment response is looking like global panic. What's interesting, *Psychology Today* points out, is that your doctor is not panicking:[69]

> COVID-19 is a new virus in a well-known class of viruses. The coronaviruses are cold viruses. I've treated countless patients with coronaviruses over the years. In fact, we've been able to test

67 Kliff, Sarah. 2020. "Kept at the Hospital on Coronavirus Fears, Now Facing Large Medical Bills." *The New York Times*, February 29.

68 See article herein entitled "Should Government Go Medieval During Pandemic Disease?"

69 Escalante, Alison. 2020. "Why Your Doctor Is Not Panicking About Novel Coronavirus." *Psychology Today*, March 4.

for them on our respiratory panels for the entirety of my career.

We know how cold viruses work: They cause runny noses, sneezing, cough, and fever, and make us feel tired and achy. For almost all of us, they run their course without medication.[70] And in the vulnerable, they can trigger a more severe illness like asthma or pneumonia.

Yes, this virus is different and worse than other coronaviruses, but it still looks very familiar. We know more about it than we don't know.

Doctors know what to do with respiratory viruses. As a pediatrician, I take care of patients with hundreds of different viruses that behave similarly to this one. We take care of the kids at home and see them if the fever is prolonged, if they get dehydrated, or if they develop breathing difficulty. Then we treat those problems and support the child until they get better.

Meanwhile, the *New England Journal of Medicine* reports as follows:[71]

On the basis of a case definition requiring a diagnosis of pneumonia, the currently reported case fatality rate is approximately 2%. In another article in the Journal, Guan et al. report mortality of 1.4% among 1,099 patients with laboratory-confirmed Covid-19; these patients had a wide spectrum of disease severity. If one

---

70 Psychology Today. N.d. "What Is Psychopharmacology?" *Psychology Today*.

71 Fauci, Anthony S., H. Clifford Lane & Robert R. Redfield. 2020. "Covid-19 — Navigating the Uncharted." *The New England Journal of Medicine*, February 28.

assumes that the number of asymptomatic or minimally symptomatic cases is several times as high as the number of reported cases, the case fatality rate may be considerably less than 1%. This suggests that the overall clinical consequences of Covid-19 may ultimately be more akin to those of a severe seasonal influenza (which has a case fatality rate of approximately 0.1%) or a pandemic influenza (similar to those in 1957 and 1968) rather than a disease similar to SARS or MERS, which have had case fatality rates of 9 to 10% and 36%, respectively.

Slate's piece on this topic offers more perspective:[72]

This all suggests that COVID-19 is a relatively benign disease for most young people, and a potentially devastating one for the old and chronically ill, albeit not nearly as risky as reported. Given the low mortality rate among younger patients with coronavirus—zero in children 10 or younger among hundreds of cases in China, and 0.2-0.4 percent in most healthy nongeriatric adults (and this is still before accounting for what is likely to be a high number of undetected asymptomatic cases)—we need to divert our focus away from worrying about preventing systemic spread among healthy people—which is likely either inevitable, or out of our control—and commit most if not all of our resources toward protecting those truly at risk of developing critical illness and even death: everyone over 70, and people who are already at higher risk from this kind of virus.

---

72 Faust, Jeremy Samuel. 2020. "COVID-19's Mortality Rate Isn't As High As We Think." *Slate*, March 4.

Look, I'm obviously not in a position to comment on the medical aspects of this; I defer to the experts.[73] But neither are medical professionals in a position to comment on the political response to this; mostly they have assiduously declined to do so.

Meanwhile, governments are willy-nilly making drastic decisions that profoundly affect the status of human freedom. Their decisions are going to affect our lives in profound ways. And there has thus far been no real debate on this. It's just been presumed that containment of the spread rather than the care of the sick is the only way forward.

What's more, we have governments all-too-willing to deploy their awesome powers to control human populations in direct response to mass public pressure based on fears that have so far not been justified by any available evidence.

Based on the Austin, Texas, precedent, any mayor of any town in America can right now declare a state of emergency, cancel events, shut malls, and close parks. Who is to stop them from shuttering stores, restaurants, schools, and churches, and quarantining whole neighborhoods?

For this reason, we have every reason to be concerned.

Are we really ready to imprison the world, wreck financial markets, destroy countless jobs, and massively disrupt life as we know it, all to forestall some uncertain fate, even as medical professionals do know the right way to deal with respiratory illness in general from a medical point of view? It's at least worth debating.

---

73 CDC. 2020. "Cases in U.S." *Centers for Disease Control and Prevention.*

ECONOMIC CRISIS IS THE STATE'S OXYGEN
BY JOHN TAMNY

March 9, 2020.

Investment powers economic growth. Period. If this statement of the obvious triggers certain readers, it's probably best for the sensitive to stop reading now.

For those not offended by the obvious, it should be said that we all have endless consumptive desires. But as individuals we all know that those desires can't be fulfilled absent production first. Consumption is a consequence of production, and investment powers production. The more investment in our capacity to produce, the more resources boosting our ability to produce, at which point our ability to consume soars.

Before tractors and fertilizer wrought by intrepid investment, most consumed very little. They did because so much of their effort was directed—often unsuccessfully—toward the mere creation of food. Thank goodness for investment. It freed people from the most menial of work that enabled microscopic amounts of consumption.

Looked at more broadly, the innovative, life-altering, growth-boosting businesses in the economy are almost invariably a consequence of wildly courageous, risk-ignoring investment. Very occasionally these bold capital allocations lead to wondrous surprises. General Electric was once just that. GE came to be because an oddball inventor by the name of Thomas Edison found a rich banking heir by the name of J.P. Morgan who rather uniquely thought the light bulb had promise. Morgan was rich, hence he had money *to lose* on something that thoroughly transformed living standards for the better, but that few believed would.

Looked at modernly, that's why a dollar in Michael Bloomberg's pocket is exponentially more growth-stimulative than a dollar in yours or mine. Bloomberg has money to *lose*. He can take huge investment risks. Goodness, he just lost $570 million on a presidential campaign. The wealth of the staggeringly rich is the most important wealth of all. *Period*. That is so precisely because the wealth of the rich can be directed to the riskiest of ventures that almost never bear fruit, but that boost productivity and living standards remarkably when they do.

Which brings us to Jason Furman's typically obtuse opinion piece in *The Wall Street Journal* last week, titled "The Case for a Big Coronavirus Stimulus." Actually Mr. Furman, it's your case. Not *the* case. The passably sentient among us wonder if there *is* a case. Needless to say, the coronavirus scare has given life to a policy crowd ever eager to centrally plan good outcomes.

In Furman's case, one supposes that the Harvard professor, because he's a Harvard professor, can afford to be ridiculous. Tenure is cushy. Unfortunately, op-eds don't create economic growth. Furman's would bring on the opposite of growth. Readers might consider this when wondering why equity markets remain volatile. Though coronavirus is priced, what the governing class will do in response *isn't*. Political action is all a speculation. Though Furman is Barack Obama's former CEA head, it's possible investors fear the Republicans (and governments around the world) coming up with stimulus ideas similar to Furman's. If so, markets would logically discount what has nothing to do with growth, and realistically has a lot to do with slower growth, in negative fashion.

First off, Furman observed that "the lower interest rates [from the Fed] and depreciated dollar will provide only modest relief after a substantial lag." Though he considers the Fed's action "bold," he fears a lag. Furman misses the point. Credit is a consequence of production. Always. We borrow money for what the money can be exchanged for. Assuming slower growth, meaning less production, there will be less credit available. The Fed can't change that, thus raising a question of what Furman means by "modest relief" from the Fed. Try none.

As for a "depreciated dollar," it's seemingly lost on Furman and President Trump that investors denominate their returns in dollars. In short, a depreciated dollar will exist as a tax on the very investment that powers economic growth. Translated, a depreciated dollar will shrink investment when more would enhance growth.

Where it gets comical is when Furman argues that "Congress should pass a simple one-time payment of $1,000 to every adult who is a U.S. citizen or a taxpaying U.S. resident, and $500 to every child who meets the same criteria." No, that's just not serious. Let's not forget that the vast majority of federal revenues come from the richest taxpayers. What this means is that Furman is calling for a massive transfer of wealth of the hundreds of billions variety from the rich to the middle class and poor. He's ignoring that unspent wealth in the hands of the rich is the most economically stimulative, company and job creating wealth of all, and it is because the rich will invest it as opposed to spending it.

Is it any wonder investors are a little bit worried? Right when investment is needed, policy types are looking to stimulate consumption. They can do no such thing as is. They can merely shift wealth from the hands of investors into the hands of consumers. The big loser in this scenario will be the economy as investment capital is shrunken by alarmist policy types.

There's that old Randolph Bourne line that war is "the health of the state." So true. In my case, and going back to the 2008 time period, I added that economic crises (real and imagined) are the state's "oxygen."

They give the Furmans of the world a voice, and a perilous one at that. Economic growth is a consequence of investment, yet Furman and all too many economists are calling for the state to stimulate consumption. You can't make this up.

Which brings us to Larry Kudlow, Trump's NEC head. Kudlow knows what works, but the job he's in forces him to play politics. So while he wisely dismissed the proverbial "helicopter drops" of money that so excite economists, he called for "targeted stimulus." One supposes here that this was the bone Kudlow threw to his boss, and a Ruling Class that lives for "crisis." That's the case simply because Kudlow knows "targeted stimulus" is what's already happening in the free marketplace *all the time*. Resources never sit idle; rather investors are relentlessly pushing them to their highest use. In short, "targeted stimulus" would in reality be the federal government doing nothing. Let market actors direct resources to where growth is optimized.

The problem is that the Ruling Classes don't seek what's best for growth. They seek what's best for them. In an eerie replay of Rahm Emanuel's line about how "you never let a crisis go to waste," Furman worried in the *Journal* about "the likelihood that history judges the economic response to coronavirus as too little and too late." Furman thinks like a policy guy. One senses Kudlow doesn't, but has to.

The losers in this are the people in the real economy who yearn for more economic growth. Growth is yet again a consequence of market-driven investment, but policymakers are calling for a huge wealth shift from investors to consumers, alongside the *politicization* of investment. Sorry, that doesn't work. Central planning that never works in boom times certainly doesn't in trying times.

Maybe the above is the message of the market at the end of last week. With the virus priced, investor are now hedging themselves against a typically obtuse and alarmist reaction from policymakers that will enhance the power of government at the expense of the private sector where all growth takes place. More government waste, fewer GEs of tomorrow. Sad.

SMALL-BUSINESS OPTIMISM REMAINED HIGH IN FEBRUARY BUT COVID-19 INCREASES UNCERTAINTY

BY ROBERT HUGHES

March 10, 2020.

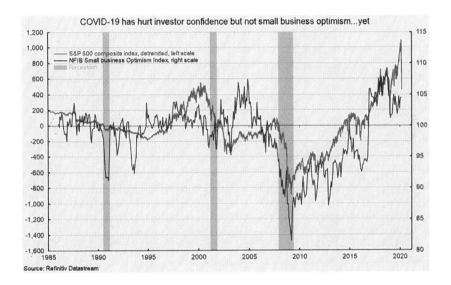

COVID-19 has hurt investor confidence but not small business optimism...yet

— S&P 500 composite index, detrended, left scale
— NFIB Small business Optimism Index, right scale
Recession

Source: Refinitiv Datastream

The small-business-optimism index from the National Federation of Independent Business rose to 104.5 in February, up 0.2 points from 104.3 in January and it is now 4.3 points below the all-time high of 108.8 in August 2018 (see chart). The latest result extends a run of 39 consecutive months above 100, averaging 104.8 over the period, a very high figure by historical comparison.

Among the key takeaways are concern over the tight labor market and the difficulty in finding qualified workers. The persistent high level of optimism stands in sharp contrast to investor optimism as reflected in the performance of the S&P 500. The popular benchmark index has declined sharply in recent weeks over fears over COVID-19 spread (see chart). The effects of the COVID-19 outbreak remain fairly limited for the small-business sector.

Within the details of the small business survey, the percentage of respondents believing now is a good time to expand came in at 26, down from 28 in January. However, the net percentage of respondents expecting better economic conditions ("better" minus "worse") came in at 22, up from 14 in January.

A net 19 percent of respondents expect higher sales over the coming months, down from 23 in January, while a net 5 percent report higher sales for the most recent three months versus the prior three months.

The percentage of firms planning to increase employment rose to 21 percent in February. A near-record 38 percent (versus a record 39 percent) of firms report having openings they are not able to fill at the moment. At the same time, the percentage of firms reporting few or no qualified applicants for job openings was 52 percent, up from 49 percent in January and now 5 points below the record 57 percent from August.

The combination of healthy labor demand and weak supply has a near-record net 36 percent of firms saying they have already increased compensation over the past three months while 19 percent intend to increase worker pay over the coming months.

The labor-market dynamics have made quality of labor the most important issue for small businesses. Among the 10 issues listed in the survey, quality of labor ranks first at 25 percent, two points below the survey high of 27 percent. Taxes were second at 14 percent while government regulation and red tape was third on the list at 13 percent. Inflation along with financing and interest rates were at the bottom of the list with just 1 percent and 2 percent of respondents identifying them as the single most important problem, respectively. Inflation has been at the bottom of the list for several years, reflecting the slow pace of price increases over the current economic cycle.

Capital expenditures by small businesses also remain solid, with 62 percent of such businesses having made capital expenditures during the past six months. That is slightly below the typical percentage in the upper 60s during the late 1990s but well above the mid-40s percentages during the last recession. Twenty-six percent of firms have plans for capital expenditures over the next three to six months, down slightly from 28 percent from the prior month. The most popular type of expenditure was equipment (43 percent) followed by vehicles (26 percent) and building/land improvement (18 percent). The most popular outlay range was $10,000 to $49,999.

Overall, the survey suggests the small-business sector of the economy remains relatively robust, with labor-market concerns holding front and center. The direct impact of the COVID-19 virus remains relatively limited for now.

THE FREE MARKET PROVIDES WHAT WE NEED TO SURVIVE A PANDEMIC
BY JEFFREY TUCKER

March 10, 2020.

What hand sanitizer you are using, where did you get it? The local store or an online shop. And who made it? Private enterprise, operating based on profit and loss within a market economy. And that mask you are keeping just in case? Same thing. It came from private investment, brought to you by international trade. It cost a buck or two but it might save your life.

Those latex gloves? An amazing innovation with a remarkable history.[74] The first ones were invented at the height of the hated Gilded Age in 1883, a result of the booming oil industry which led to countless derivative products. Disposable versions are wonderfully sanitary but they have only been available since 1964, as innovated by the private company Ansell, founded by Eric Ansell in Melbourne, Australia. Thank you international trade.

That food you are stockpiling, who is selling you that? It's the local grocery or perhaps a big-box discount store that allows you to purchase vast quantities at a discount. The bottled water you now have, thank the merchant who eschews municipal water while knowing that people expect better.

The equipment at the hospital that will keep you breathing and medicated is manufactured by private enterprise. I can't think of a single exception. You don't seriously think that the Centers for Disease

---

74 2012. "History of Latex Gloves." *Cascade Healthcare Solutions*, May 4.

Control makes heart monitors and respirators, do you?

And the information you are getting on the latest virus updates, what is delivering it to you?

Most likely the world wide web, made possible by private servers, given to you on privately owned fiber-optics cables, flowing to your privately made and distributed computer or smartphone, which today is more capable than the supercomputers of 20 years ago, thanks to the driving force of the market to innovate in service of the common person.

Or maybe you are watching a 72-inch television that you picked up for $1000 at Costco to deliver a home-viewing experience not even the richest person would have enjoyed 15 years ago.

And that house right now where you have decided to quarantine yourself, who built that? Who made the materials possible? You owe it all to private business operating within a market framework, real estate developers who face a daily test of their wherewithal by facing brutal competition. Your home is insured by private companies who bear all the risk of disaster so that you don't have to.

Who is innovating the home-testing kits that are now reaching people in areas most affected? It's the Bill & Melinda Gates Foundation as funded by the hated billionaire capitalist who turned his wealth into global philanthropy to fight diseases just like this one.[75] Here is private enterprise at work.

The truth is that the market loves you right now, more in the midst of a

---

75 Doughton, Sandi. 2020. "Gates-funded program will soon offer home-testing kits for new coronavirus." *The Seattle Times*, March 8.

disease panic than ever before.[76] It would love you even more if companies were not being browbeat by government into curbing sales of essential items. Let the prices of sanitizer and masks rise and you draw more into production and distribution. Throttle the market and you reduce supply.

The market would have loved you more had the Centers for Disease Control not failed to authorize private companies to test for the virus. It was only after the aggressive protests of the governor of New York that the CDC gave in and let people do what they wanted to do.[77]

And what is the mighty contribution of government these days? To order quarantines but not to tell you whether you can step outside, how you will get groceries, how long it will last, who you can invite in, and when it will all end. Don't try to call the authorities. They have better and bigger things to worry about than your sorry plight that is causing you sleepless nights and endless worry. Thank goodness for digital technology that allows you to communicate with friends and family.

How many times have you heard something of the following?

"I would take advantage of these low-priced fares and cheap hotels, but I'm afraid of getting quarantined."

Think what this statement means. It means that people are more afraid of their own governments than they are of COVID-19. How is that making a contribution to getting through this sad stage of history?

And so, given all of this, it appalls me that the bitter-fingered pundits type up articles trashing the market as nothing but a Trumpish plot to

---

76 Tucker, Jeffrey A. 2019. *The Market Loves You: Why You Should Love It Back*. Published by American Institute for Economic Research: Great Barrington, MA.

77 De Freytas-Tamura, Kimiko. 2020. "Cuomo Attacks C.D.C. Over Delays in Coronavirus Testing." *The New York Times*, March 8.

pillage you whereas government is saving you. I waited for days and weeks for someone finally to say what so many wanted to say, which is that "there are no libertarians in an epidemic."[78]

On the contrary, it is human liberty operating within a market framework that saves us in times like this.

In a disease panic, we are learning, people lose their minds and stop thinking clearly about things that matter. They also reach out to authority to save them. All of this is expected. And it's very sad. Even sadder is how the unscrupulous power mongers among us use such times to enhance the power of the state over our lives and claim it is for our own good.

We should expect more of our public intellectuals than to use this tragedy to trash market-based institutions that are working 24/7 to provide you and your loved ones what you need to survive this mess. When it's the difference between health and sickness, life and death, government is the last institution you want to trust.

78 Nicholas, Peter. 2020. "There Are No Libertarians in an Epidemic." *The Atlantic*, March 10.

THEY ARE REWRITING THE HISTORY OF CORONAVIRUS IN REAL TIME
BY PETER C. EARLE

March 11, 2020.

What is the story of the coronavirus, the market crash, and the economic upheaval that will likely follow? The pundit and intellectual classes are hard at work to tell the story in a way that confirms their ideological biases. Their message: in times when everyone turned against the public sector, with budget and staffing cuts, we learned that only the government can save us from a worse calamity.

Let this be a lesson unto us all! Or maybe not.

The storyline is not unlike the one they tell about the Great Depression and the Crash of 2008. The market was unstable, overly exuberant, and animated by "greed," and the super rich were running wild, so of course the crash came, just as hell is the destination of the sinful. Then our government officials and charges, wise and brave, rode in on a white horse and cleaned up the place, instituted controls, and put history back on the right course.

The elements of the evolving account aren't true, but they make for a pleasant fiction for the ideologically minded. Of course, Herbert Hoover was not a "do nothing" president; of course, Bill Clinton didn't "balance the budget."[79]

Something in this same revisionist tradition is taking place before our very eyes. The coronavirus is penance for market-oriented sins,

79 Klein, Christopher. 2019. "Before FDR, Herbert Hoover Tried His Own 'New Deal'." *History.com*, February 28; Moore, Stephen. 1998. "No, Bill Clinton Didn't Balance the Budget." *Cato Institute*, October 8.

but the hallowed halls of government are forgiving and coming to our rescue.

WEAVING THE NARRATIVE

For example, a popular talking point at present is that the Trump administration deeply slashed funding for the Centers for Disease Control, and consequently the government response to the coronavirus has been slower and less effective than it would have been otherwise. The mainstream media, the two most prominent remaining Democratic presidential hopefuls, and a smattering of other public intellectuals have thrown this claim around as well. In fact, the administration proposed sweeping cuts not only to the CDC but also the National Institute of Health, but neither were approved by Congress.

Nor does it follow that cuts to any particular branch of government would necessarily have led to a delayed or less effective response to this or any other public health hazard. In fact, the Centers for Disease Control's budget was at its lowest in 2013, and throughout the current administration's tenure it has been in line with average budget levels over the last decade, with the exception of 2018, at which point it was at its highest.[80]

It is true that certain members of pandemic response teams were fired (or resigned—another detail glazed over) over the last two years, but there, too, it does not necessarily follow that this made the response to the outbreak of coronavirus—which initially took place in China, whose massive legions of state bureaucrats, near-total control of society,

---

80 McKillop M, Ilakkuvan V. The Impact of Chronic Underfunding on America's Public Health System: Trends, Risks, and Recommendations, 2019. TFAH. April 2019.

and considerable resources couldn't get the outbreak under control either - more ineffective than it would have been otherwise.[81] And in fact, the specific timing of the exit of those individuals seems to have had more to do with the sudden arrival of John Bolton and a planned restructuring of the National Security Council.

It's also no big surprise that numerous government positions have remained empty during the current administration: that has as much to do with congressional foot-dragging and with rapid turnover in certain offices as it does the administration's stated goal of trimming the size of government.[82] But despite media (and congressional) claims of disruption, American life seems suspiciously none the worse for wear.[83] It's difficult to read an editorial that warns of "the dangers of an acting official" without snickering.[84]

And yet among millions, and perhaps tens of millions, of people a fable has coalesced: that deep budget cuts and a winnowing of experts by an ostensibly free market leaning administration have led to the more rapid spread of the coronavirus (and its consequent effects on the word economy). It has become the story, stolid and inviolable.

Make no mistake: some people will vote based upon this chronicling of events. These anecdotes, undeniably false, will nevertheless

---

81 Fabian, Jordan & Katie Bo Williams. 2018. "Bolton not done resetting Trump national security team." *The Hill*, April 15.

82 Gregorian, Dareh. 2019. "Help Wanted: Trump administration riddled with vacancies." *NBC News*, March 28.

83 Thomsen (2018); Reed, Brad. 2019. "Republican senators concerned that President Donald Trump has "too many" vacancies in his Cabinet." *Salon*, February 4.

84 Lu, Chris. 2019. "Why Trump's Cabinet vacancies, turnover threaten our government." *USA Today*, April 17.

appear in books, editorials, and other historical depictions of the current era. They will be taught to children, and through the process of second-hand dealing in ideas over time will be woven into the fabric of the zeitgeist. In ten or twenty years it will have become part of the received knowledge of pundits, amateur and expert alike.

A HOAX OF HOAXES

Another widely held assertion is that, early on, President Trump referred to the coronavirus itself as a "hoax." In fact, at a February 28 campaign rally in South Carolina he referred to criticism of the administration's handling of the still-nascent pandemic as "the new hoax," suggesting (cogently) that it was yet another attempt, following the Mueller Report and the thwarted impeachment campaign, to impugn his policies and prevent his re-election.

And there have been others: a national emergency (with all of its unseemly accoutrements) was, contrary to other tellings, declared before there was a single coronavirus death within the United States.[85] And comparing the US (read: Trump's) response to the pandemic to that of Switzerland, a country with 2.6 percent of the population and 0.4 percent of the landmass of the United States, is nothing short of risible.

In fact, there's nothing particularly abnormal about the delays and missteps the current administration has demonstrated; subpar preparedness is a part of the political endeavor, regardless of

---

85 Jackson, David. 2020. "Trump administration declares coronavirus emergency, orders first quarantine in 50 years." *USA Today*, January 31; Aubrey, Allison. 2020. "Trump Declares Coronavirus A Public Health Emergency And Restricts Travel From China." *NPR*, January 31.

the party in power.[86] Yet in real time, a subplot is being rewritten and served wholesale to hundreds of millions of people: virally, indeed.

In fact—long forgotten and absent from the prevailing account of the previous administration's handling—six years after the original H1N1 outbreak, a serious resurgence took place.[87]

There have been loose statements made that can be taken several ways.[88] Big surprise: Trump makes wild, offhand comments vastly outside of his core competencies. That's less revelation than landscape by now, and it isn't unique to the current chief executive either—although he has undoubtedly made more of a habit of it than any other president in modern history.[89]

POST-TRUTH, POST-FACT

The fact is, if Donald Trump is the first "post-truth" president, he hasn't been alone in crafting the workings of this era: the post-fact media and intelligentsia preceded him by decades. Misrepresentations, skewed reporting, and a prevailing inclination to accept news that buttresses one's ideology while discarding, or labeling false, any contraindications are now the prevailing condition.

---

86 CNN. 2009. "Obama declares H1N1 emergency." *CNN*, October 26; Osterholm, Michael T. 2007. "Unprepared for a Pandemic." *Foreign Affairs*, March/April; McNiel Jr, Donald G. 2009. "Shortages and Confusion in the Flu Fight." October 23.

87 Davlin, Stacy L., Lenee Blanton, Krista Kniss et al. 2016. "Influenza Activity — United States, 2015–16 Season and Composition of the 2016–17 Influenza Vaccine." *CDC*, Morbidity and Mortality Weekly Report 65.

88 Rieder, Rem. 2020. "Trump and the Coronavirus Death Rate." *FactCheck. org*, March 5.

89 Ross, Brian, Alex Hosenball, Cho Park & Lee Ferran. 2016. "ISIS 2 Years Later: From 'JV Team' to International Killers." *ABC News*, June 29.

It was just reported that New York State will activate the National Guard and deploy it to New Rochelle to "contain" the city. Will the media and the scolding class, always poised to pounce on the mere suggestion that government isn't always the answer, report the most salient element of this development, which is that to the outside (or, more aptly, inside) observer enforced quarantine and "containment centers" bear an uncanny likeness to martial law?[90]

The story that is being woven before our eyes is the opposite of the truth. Average people fear the quarantine more than the virus, and rationally so. Restrictions on travel increase public panic. The dictatorial canceling of events (and the mimicking of those cancellations to signal vigilance) has devastated hotels, airlines, restaurants, and destinations. The daily threats and warnings have spooked markets far more than the sober analysis from genuine medical professionals. Markets, non-interventionist policies, and budget cuts have between little and nothing to do with the fear now spreading.

---

90 Millman, Jennifer. 2020. "NJ Announces 1st COVID-19 Death; NY Deploys National Guard to New Rochelle." *NBC New York*, March 11; Higgins-Dunn, Noah & William Feuer. 2020. "New York Gov. Cuomo deploys National Guard to New Rochelle, establishes containment center to stem coronavirus." *CNBC News,* March 10.

BE ALARMED, BUT DON'T PANIC
BY STEPHEN DAVIES

March 12, 2020.

In the last few decades there have been a succession of panics, each of which has for a while attracted much attention, been taken seriously by much of the media and even parts of academia, and in some cases influenced public policy. One fondly remembered example was the Y2K panic in which it was thought that the advent of the millennium would result in the general collapse of computers and automated systems due to a design fault in their operating software and mechanics. Another was the belief that temperate forests and waterways would be wiped out by acid rain. Both of those faded away, rather suddenly in the case of Y2K.

Others recur such as the notion that we are all suffering a range of mysterious ailments because of the accumulation of 'artificial' toxins in our bodies—this one gets an outing every few years. There are some panics that never really get off the ground, such as the idea that the wireless transmissions of the mobile telephone system are causing widespread health problems. While there is no shortage of this, panic debunkers such as the British peer and writer Matt Ridley have a fulltime job on their hands debunking them.

However, it is illogical and dangerous to conclude that because most scares turn out to be without foundation we should therefore reject any such alarms. Sometimes the problem is genuine, and we should indeed be concerned. In some of those cases there is a relatively simple solution: this was the case with the damage to the Earth's ozone layer for example. More serious are cases where the problem is real, is severe or potentially severe, and does not have an easy solution. In those cases we should be alarmed, indeed very alarmed.

A few years ago a then-colleague of mine asked me if we should be concerned about the problem of antibiotic resistance in bacteria. She expected me to say this was nothing to worry about and was dismayed when I told her I thought it was a serious problem with potentially far-reaching effects. Right now we are confronted with another such case, of a problem where we really should be worried—as Matt Ridley himself has recently said.[91]

This is of course the coronavirus outbreak, almost certainly now a true pandemic. Ridley explains why the biology of the virus and the way we live today both mean that this is a threat we should take very seriously. The boy may have been crying wolf repeatedly but eventually the wolf really did come. This time it truly has and we do not yet know how badly we shall be bitten.

Biology and epidemiology and medicine are obviously the disciplines that can help us to best evaluate the risks posed by a pandemic, and to devise the most effective response. In this case, as Ridley explains, the heart of the challenge is that we are dealing with a new virus that has not yet adapted to its host (us) by becoming milder and which currently has the dark combination of a long incubation period, high levels of infectiousness, and a relatively high mortality rate.

All this explains why it is a real problem and a serious one. To understand why this is happening now though, and to have a better grasp of what the non-medical consequences might be if we are not careful, we should turn to the disciplines of history and economics

---

91 Ridley, Matt. 2020. "Coronavirus is the wolf on the loose." *Matt Ridley*, March 10.

and their combination in economic history.

Epidemics are a regularly recurring feature of human history. Some are regular, even annual. Most are localised. Some though are major events, with epidemics that affect a significant part of the planet's surface and settled population or even the entire settled world (a pandemic). These often have extensive and long-lasting consequences and can be seen with hindsight or even at the time to have played a major part in history. Such major epidemics and pandemics do not, however, happen randomly and unpredictably, without any warning.

They are not 'black swan events,' which are unknowable and unpredictable. Rather, they are 'grey swans'—we can work out what circumstances make them more likely but the problem is that we cannot say precisely when or where they will happen. For the economist the analysis of the historians on this topic is sobering but it also suggests warnings about what to do and not to do.

Historically, pandemics and epidemics that affect a large part of the planet and its population tend to happen towards the end of long periods of economic growth, increased trade and urbanisation, and a move towards significant economic integration and division of labor. They typically happen in, and have the biggest impact upon, the parts of the world where those processes were most sustained and advanced.

At a theoretical level this makes sense. Trade and economic specialisation means lots of goods and people moving around, along with parasites, pathogens, and hosts such as rats. The more trade and economic integration there is, the easier it is for a novel pathogen to travel long distances and infect large numbers of people over a wide area.

The urbanisation that goes along with economic development means large and concentrated populations (often historically with inadequate sanitation) make the spread of a disease much easier and means that a true epidemic (in which until the peak is reached each case gives rise to at least two new ones, so producing exponential growth) is much more likely. So major epidemics are the dark consequence of good things such as economic development and the growth of trade and exchange.

We can see this clearly if we look at some of the best-known major epidemics and pandemics. The influenza epidemic of 1918 happened not just at the end of a world war but at the close of a 40-year episode of globalisation (the so-called 'Belle Epoque'). The Black Death, a true pandemic that wiped out about half of the population of Eurasia in the fourteenth century, came at the end of another 200-year period of intensifying trade and exchange connections between the various parts of Eurasia, particularly in the thirteenth century after the Mongols had united most of it in the vast empire of Genghis Khan and his successors.

The ever closer integration of the lands around the Mediterranean and most of the Middle East in the first and second centuries (with a network of trade connections between those lands and both East and South Asia and deepening links within both of those regions) came to an abrupt halt with the massive plagues of the third century, which had a devastating effect on both the Roman and the Han Chinese Empires.

The recovery of the later fourth and fifth century was then followed by the great Plague of Justinian, which laid waste to urban society around the Mediterranean and carried off a large part of the population of both the East Roman and Sasanian Empires. In all of these cases, soldiers and merchants were among the most important transmitters of the diseases and we can trace how the epidemics spread along long-distance trade routes.

So past experience and the biology of the coronavirus should both lead us to be very alarmed. This time something really bad is coming down—we do not yet know how bad (although it will not have the catastrophic results of the Black Death or Justinian's Plague). History though should have told us to be worried about something like this for some time now, and to prepare for it or take pre-emptive action. To be fair many governments and their scientific advisors have been quietly worried about this for some time (as they also are about antibiotic resistance) and there have been contingency plans which they can now test.

The problem is that several features of the way we live at the moment make major epidemics or even pandemics more likely than they would otherwise be. The principal one has already been alluded to—increased economic integration. The problem is that this means a lot more travelling and people moving around. The key factor here is not so much the number of people moving in a given time or the distances they travel on average (although both of these do matter for epidemiology) but rather the number of journeys, which is larger than the number of people because of the relatively small number of people who make frequent journeys.

In previous epidemics it was soldiers, sailors, and merchants who spread the illnesses and disproportionately died from them—we may have to add other categories now such as conference-attending academics. Urbanisation also makes large-scale outbreaks of infectious diseases easier. The other big factor is the way modern agriculture works, above all livestock farming which is a fertile ground for the development of novel pathogens and their jumping across species barriers. So, the way the world economy has developed in the last few decades has actually heightened the risk of a pandemic, particularly when coupled with other factors such as modern farming.

So we should have been worried for some time, should be alarmed now, and should be very alarmed if the exponential spread of the coronavirus continues much longer. What we should not do is panic.

The natural human response to an epidemic is to panic and to engage in various kinds of behaviour that are not helpful and may make the situation even worse—such as running away. In his Peloponnesian War, Thucydides gives a gripping account of the plague that visited Athens during the war and captures the psychological effects of the epidemic as well as its physical ones. His account is worth reading again to see what social effects a pandemic may produce.[92] The major epidemics just described did not only come towards the end of episodes of economic development—they also brought them to a close.

It is very unlikely that the coronavirus itself will do that this time for two reasons: it is not as lethal as the bubonic plague; and modern sanitation and medical knowledge and technology gives us an advantage our ancestors did not have.

What is quite possible though is that we will panic and react in the wrong way at the policy level in a way that future historians will critically analyze as an era of globalisation and world growth abruptly ended not by the illness itself but by an ill-judged response to it.

The immediate risk is that, taken together, the epidemic and the steps taken to contain it will push the world economy into a severe recession. We must obviously follow the advice of medical professionals and one of the issues they draw attention to is that many actions the public (and politicians) think will help may actually not be very useful, while having bad economic results. It may also lay bare problems that have nothing to do with it, such as the derangement of investment markets and risk pricing brought about by over a decade of 'unorthodox'

92 Wikisource. 2018. "History of the Peloponnesian War." *Wikisource*, March 20.

monetary policy.

The great danger though is that it will give a huge push and impetus to something we can already see starting, which is a move away from economic integration and towards localism and economic nationalism. Just as in the 1930s this will not end well. What, though, about the genuine heightening of risk brought about by economic integration and the more frequent travelled closer connections that it brings? The answer is that there are all kinds of things we can do and should be doing to manage, mitigate, and even eliminate those risks.

Matt Ridley points to some of them in his piece that I have referred to. Some of what we should be doing is strategic and proactive, such as encouraging the development of synthetic meat and alternatives to intensive farming. Another is developing more effective treatments for both viral and bacterial diseases (the latter involving dealing with the other rising problem of antibiotic resistance by developing things such as designed bacteriophages).

If we realise what the real risks are and take effective action that makes use of the advantages we have compared to our ancestors then we can survive a major pandemic. If we panic, however, and do things that seem to make sense but actually make the economic and social effects worse, then the prospects are bad.

CORONAVIRUS AND A CASE FOR OPTIMISM
BY BRETT DALTON AND BRUCE YANDLE

March 12, 2020.

With coronavirus fears accelerating and nations and organizations across the world grappling with how best to contain and mitigate the harm, it becomes increasingly difficult to be optimistic about the immediate future. What are the prospects for the American public and for the 2020 economy? Will we see a sharp and extended increase in sickness and fatalities? Will we observe a sleepwalking economy with hardly any GDP growth? Might we experience one of the more serious recessions of the last 20 years?

Well, we are cautiously optimistic. We are trained economists rather than public health professionals, but our backgrounds lead us to think that coronavirus will rise and fall relatively quickly and that the nation's GDP growth will mirror those effects. Look for growth to fall significantly in 2020's first half, maybe becoming negative, but rise again and recover as the year progresses. No, we do not expect to see 3.0 percent GDP growth any time soon, but look forward to seeing 2.0 percent growth again at the end of this year.

Optimistic? Some might call us irrational or something even worse. But following the extraordinary thoughts of Matt Ridley's 2010 book, "The Rational Optimist," we are convinced that markets—to the extent they are allowed to operate—working together with high-speed communications technologies, will significantly reduce the harm that could befall us.[93] Let us explain.

Make no mistake about it: We face a serious health threat and should all follow the advice and counsel of the Centers for Disease Control (CDC) and our health professionals.[94] But interestingly enough, projections from epidemiologists indicate this could be the first global pandemic in the age of the smartphone, artificial intelligence, ubiquitous cellular and internet connectedness, and globally connected communities through social media. As a result, society is better prepared to deal with a serious health threat than ever before.

So while the virus is already resulting in significant disruption, loss, and real tragedy, yes, there is cause for some optimism in times such as this. Enhanced by ubiquitous, unprecedented, and rapidly improving and inexpensive technology, we can bring innovative solutions to bear on this serious problem.

A COMPARISON WITH EARLIER PANDEMICS:

Let's consider a few observations from the first two pandemics of the 21st century: severe acute respiratory syndrome (SARS) in 2002 and the "swine flu" (H1N1) in 2009. In the case of SARS, five months elapsed before the World Health Organization (WHO) and CDC issued global alerts. The Canadian Global Public Health Intelligence Network (CGPHIN) picked up information from Chinese message boards indicating a novel flu-like illness in November 2002. This information was not translated to English by the WHO and made available until January

---

93 Ridley, Matt. 2010. *The Rational Optimist: How Prosperity Evolves.* HarperCollins Publishers.

94 CDC. 2020. "Coronavirus (COVID-19)." *Centers for Disease Control and Prevention.*

21, 2003—primarily due to systems and technological limitations. It took five months to definitively identify the virus. The pandemic was contained before an actual vaccine was developed.

In the case of H1N1, the first flu pandemic in 40 years, the development of improved technology and related advances allowed for improved public health response times, more rapid genome sequencing, and advanced clinical trials and vaccine development and availability. Notably, clinical vaccine trials were underway within five months of the outbreak.

In the case of the coronavirus, a cluster of pneumonia-like illnesses were reported in the Wuhan province of China in late December 2019, with a declaration by China to the WHO on December 31. Within 24 hours, the source of the outbreak had been identified, and the virus was definitively identified by January 7. By January 9, two days before the first death, the genome of the coronavirus had been sequenced.

The first case was reported in the United States on January 21, with CDC test kits available by January 27. Less than a month later, multiple pharmaceutical companies and health research organizations had begun the clinical vaccine trial process. A vaccine developed by Moderna Therapeutics was initially sent to the National Institute of Allergy and Infectious Diseases (NIAID) on February 24, less than two months after the identification of the virus half a world away.

HOW COMMUNICATIONS LINKAGES HAVE EXPANDED:

Next, let's look at some improvements the market has delivered from the time of SARS, to H1N1, and now the coronavirus. In 2002, only 59 percent of the U.S. population had access to the internet, growing to 76 percent by 2009 and 90 percent by 2019.[95] Home broadband use increased from only 9.0 percent in January 2002 to 73 percent in February 2019.

Equally important in this case are mobile device and social media use. In 2002, the current conception of social media didn't really exist. The percent of the U.S. population using social media in 2008-09 was approximately 10 percent, ballooning to nearly 80 percent by 2019.[96] In 2002 there were no mobile devices for internet access. In 2011, only 35 percent of the U.S. population had access to mobile devices, with 81 percent having access by 2019. Nearly every American who desires internet access, social media access, and a mobile device now has it. What does this mean for core societal functions like education in the event of coronavirus-inspired disruptions? Consider that in 2002-03, only 30 percent of public K-12 school districts offered online learning options, growing to 53 percent by 2009 and 75 percent by 2013-14.[97] It is estimated that nearly all U.S. public schools now have online courses. In just the past week, we have seen major universities such as Stanford, MIT, and the University of Washington adjust and innovate to continue operations while simultaneously protecting against the spread of the virus. At the University of Washington, all spring quarter classes have been moved online.

Across the globe, we are shifting to virtual meetings, telepresence,

95 Pew Research Center. 2019. "Internet/Broadband Fact Sheet." *Pew Research Center*, June 12.

96 Pew Research Center. 2019. "Social Media Fact Sheet." Pew Research Center, June 12.

97 NCES. n.d. "Distance learning." *National Center for Education Statistics*; Connections Academy. N.d. "Infographic: Growth of K-12 Digital Learning." *Connections Academy*.

and other remote solutions to limit the risk of disease transmission. All of these advances are contributing to a future in which public health can be better protected, while simultaneously sustaining important economic and societal functions.

WHAT ABOUT CHINA, THE CORONAVIRUS EPICENTER?

China, with Earth's largest population and second-largest economy, is worth its own look. In 2009, an estimated 28 percent of Chinese citizens had internet access, increasing to 54 percent in 2017, with rates over 70 percent in major population centers. There are now more internet users in China than in any other country. 98.6 percent of Chinese users access the internet through mobile devices. Only 26 percent of Chinese citizens were using social media in 2013, growing to 60 percent by 2016.[98] Going forward, even with government intervention, it is difficult to conceive of a situation in which important public health information is unavailable or delayed to the extent that it has been during previous periods like SARS and H1N1.

Not only is access to technology significantly greater, but the power and capacity of technology is increasing exponentially. The world is quickly transforming from a 4G to a 5G platform, which is said to deliver 50 times faster speed, 10 times less latency, and 1,000 times the capacity of 4G.[99] We have yet to fully tap its potential, but the implications for artificial intelligence, public health, commerce, and

---

98 Poushter, Jacob, Caldwell Bishop & Hanyu Chwe. 2018. "Social Media Use Continues to Rise in Developing Countries but Plateaus Across Developed Ones." Pew Research Center, June 19.

99 Ericsson. 2019. "Ericsson Mobility Report: 5G uptake even faster than expected." *Ericsson*, press release June 11; Intel. n.d. "The 5G Effect: Your 5G Business Opportunity." *Intel*, infographic.

education are significant—perhaps signaling even greater optimism that we can fight a future outbreak.

FINAL THOUGHTS

Coronavirus is deadly. We have not yet come close to solving the problem and must take it seriously. But better information is leading to public health improvements in early detection, screening, treatment, education, disease containment, mobilization of medical resources, rapid data capture and analysis, as well as rapid and effective vaccine development and delivery. More broadly, improvements are being developed in supply chains, manufacturing solutions, virtual organizational structures, business continuity strategies, online education, and the list goes on.

Most are market-driven technological advances to meet basic and simple incentives stemming from consumers' needs. As a society, we would be wise to support regulatory and policy innovations which reward the continued development and dissemination of technological advances, drug development and dissemination, the free and unfiltered access and exchange of information, alternative education delivery methods and nimble and flexible approaches to challenges of all sorts.

We can't change the fact that the coronavirus is here, but we can be optimistic that people (the greatest natural resource on Earth) will learn, adjust, create, innovate, and ultimately manage this problem and create lasting improvements as a result. At the present time, the most productive course of action is to heed the advice of the experts—while maintaining our rational sense of optimism rooted in a proven history of human innovation, creativity, and hard work. Let's wash our hands, take time away as needed, and get back to work.

THE FED CANNOT COMBAT CORONAVIRUS
BY SCOTT A. BURNS

March 5, 2020.

At a campaign speech on February 29, Senator Elizabeth Warren (D-Mass.) introduced her economic plan for combating COVID-19, more commonly known as the coronavirus.[100]

The Warren plan has two elements. First, it calls for "a major targeted fiscal stimulus" to counteract the negative economic effects of the coronavirus. In particular, she calls for the federal government to "provide direct support to businesses of all sizes that have seen their supply chains disrupted." Second, and more controversial, her plan calls on "the Federal Reserve to take action to help out American companies."

"During the financial crisis, the Fed quietly gave big banks access to trillions of dollars in low-cost loans to prop them up," Warren said. Building on this crisis-era policy, she proposed that "the Fed should stand ready to offer low-cost loans to companies that agree to support their workers and that need a little help to make it through the next few months."

President Trump has also made it clear that he would like the Fed to intervene to combat the coronavirus. "I hope the Fed gets involved, and I hope they get involved soon," he told White House reporters last Friday. But this is hardly a departure from his usual calls for the Fed to lower interest rates in an effort to boost economic growth.

---

100 Wrigley, Deborah. 2020. "Elizabeth Warren lays out plan to fight coronavirus at Houston town hall." March 4.

Trump's pressure on the Fed isn't wise. But Warren's proposal goes much further in the wrong direction by calling on the Fed to expand its controversial, preferential lending.

Warren's plan is dangerously wrong on many fronts. It presumes the Fed's response to the financial crisis is worth emulating. It's true that the Fed, in its role as a lender of last resort, should provide enough liquidity during financial panics to stabilize total spending and prevent the unnecessary tidal wave of bank failures that were experienced during the Great Depression.

Providing liquidity to solvent but illiquid banks at above-market interest rates on good collateral, as Walter Bagehot famously prescribed, is advisable. But this is a far cry from what the Fed actually did—providing sterilized loans to dozens of potentially insolvent banks at below-market interest on bad collateral.[101] Contrary to popular belief, there is no compelling evidence that these actions did anything but prop up poorly run institutions and generate moral hazard for decades to come.[102]

In suggesting that the Fed should extend low-interest loans to *nonbanks*, Warren's proposal is potentially even more dangerous. It's true that, during the Great Recession, the Fed used its emergency powers to extend loans to nontraditional banks in the shadow banking sector. Whether these actions were warranted or within its mandate

---

101 Bagehot, Walter. 1873. *Lombard Street: A Description of the Money Market*; Selgin, George. 2012. "L Street: Bagehotian Prescriptions for a 21st Century Money Market." *Cato Journal*, 32(2): 303-332.

102 White, Lawrence H. 2016. "Needed: A Federal Reserve Exit from Preferential Credit Allocation." *Cato Journal*, 36(2): 353-365.

remains controversial.[103] But, at least in those cases, the Fed could plausibly argue that it was acting in line with its original mission. It has no authority to provide bailouts to firms outside the financial sector.

Warren's plan highlights the dangers of blurring the lines between monetary and fiscal policy. As Lawrence White and I recently argued in the *Cato Journal*, offering subsidies and bailouts to specific firms and sectors isn't monetary policy—as it "neither aims to provide liquidity to the financial system as a whole, nor to alter the trajectory of the money supply to achieve macroeconomic objectives."[104] It is fiscal policy masquerading as monetary policy.

Politicians should not be able to offload fiscal policies on the Fed. If they want to conduct fiscal policy, let them do so in the open, so that their actions might be judged by voters. We certainly do not want politicians to view the Fed as merely an extension of the Treasury, as it once was. If they do, we would lose the modest bit of central bank independence gained over the last seven decades in a sneeze—and, with it, any hope for sound monetary policy divorced from shortsighted politicians.

Ultimately, Warren's coronavirus plan is just the latest symptom of a disease afflicting monetary discourse: the ever-increasing politicization of monetary policy. One can hardly blame Warren for wanting to use the Fed to conduct fiscal policy. The Fed's emergency lending powers have, in fact, been used and abused in this way in the not-so-distant

---

103 Blinder, Alan S. 2010. "Quantitative Easing: Entrance and Exit Strategies." *Federal Reserve Bank of St. Louis Review*, 96(2): 465-480.

104 Burns, Scott A. & Lawrence H. White. 2019. "Political Economy of the Fed's Unconventional Monetary and Credit Policies." *Cato Journal*, 39(2): 369-381.

past. If enacted, her plan would represent another big step toward breaking down the quarantine wall that separates monetary and fiscal policy. But it would hardly be the first step.

SOUTH KOREA PRESERVED THE OPEN SOCIETY AND NOW INFECTION RATES ARE FALLING
BY PETER C. EARLE

March 12, 2020.

What's better for dealing with pandemic disease: martial-law quarantines imposed by the state according to geography, or keeping society open while trusting medical professionals, individuals, families, and communities to make intelligent decisions?

A month ago, such a question would have been purely hypothetical but the answer in the United States would have been settled. After all, this is a country of law, with a Bill of Rights, limits on state power, and an essential trust in freedom. Right?

How times change in a crisis. Mayors and governors around the country are imposing quarantines, not because they work but because they don't want to be blamed for failing to act. So let's consider that essential question: what works?

South Korea has seen a steady decrease in new coronavirus cases for the latter half of the last week. The country had the fourth most cases of coronavirus in the world. There were no geographic quarantines enforced by armed guards. Instead, the sole focus was on widespread testing and isolating the sick.

After averaging over 500 new cases per day back to the last week of February, between Friday and Sunday the daily totals numbered

438,367, and 248 according to the Korea Centers for Disease Control.[105]

How is it that without deploying the military or imposing widespread, enforced quarantine, the spread of coronavirus in South Korea is apparently slowing?

ACTUALLY, THERE'S A BETTER QUESTION: WHY SHOULD THE U.S. COPY CHINA RATHER THAN SOUTH KOREA?

The United States is deep in the throes of an election season at present, and so haughty invokings of the Constitution and Declaration of Independence are recurrent (if not always coherent).[106] Of course, talk is generally cheap—and all the cheaper when coming from the mouths of politicians. It's in times of crisis that the veracity of one's commitment to liberty and human rights is laid bare. The difference between the U.S. and China is that China makes no pretense of reverence for liberty, nor for the inviolate elevation of individual rights.

South Korea is leveraging private property rights to thwart the spread of the virus, with building owners posting and enforcing "no mask, no entry" signs. (Just imagine how many Americans would react to being turned away or denied service from a favored destination at

---

105 Park, Chan-kyong. 2020. "Coronavirus: South Korea's infection rate falls without citywide lockdowns like China, Italy." *South China Morning Post*, March 10.

106 2020. "Joe Biden forgets the Declaration of Independence." *Youtube*, March 3.

the sole discretion of the proprietor.[107])

Drive-through testing stations have been set up nationwide through which individuals, after a ten-minute test, are notified within a few hours if infected. A voluntary, self-diagnosis phone app was created in the early stages of the pandemic, and "living and treatment" centers set up in a "soft quarantine" spirit.

Mostly, though, South Koreans are acting based upon their experience with the H1N1 pandemic in 2009: they're washing their hands frequently, making an effort not to touch their faces, wearing masks, and social distancing to the extent possible. The high level of personal technology access in South Korea makes the lattermost eminently practicable, given the ubiquity of video telecommunications and other such technology.

Contrast this with developments in the few days since Italy put its entire country under quarantine, active cases have risen from between 5,000 and 6,000 to over 8,500. Deaths from the coronavirus have risen in that same time period from 366 to 631 (all figures as of March 10th).[108]

---

107 The Associated Press. 2019. "Woman drives motorhome into casino after she's kicked out." *NBC News*, October 25; WTOC. 2006. "Concert Goers Riot After Entry Denied." *WTOC,* July 10; Pratt, Denver. 2020. "Man who threw dog against wall after being denied entry to Bellingham bar gets jail time." *The Bellingham Herald*, March 1; Hershberg, Mark. 2019. "Broadway Theater Stands Up to Serial Suer And Wins." *Forbes*, November 30; n.d. "Man kicked out of all-you-can-eat buffet after eating more than 50 lbs of food, sues for $2 million." *World News Daily Report*; Miller, Jessica. 2013. "Utah man sues Sugar House library after being told he stinks." *The Salt Lake Tribune*, December 5; Yin, Alice. 2019. "Man shot outside Dolton Burger King after irate gunman denied drive-through service, authorities say." *Chicago Tribune*, December 19; Berhow, Josh. 2019. "Golfer sues one of world's most exclusive clubs claiming he was kicked out for playing too often." *Golf*, November 14.

108 Worldometer. 2020. "Coronavirus Cases: Italy." *Worldometer.*

It is true that certain aspects of South Korea's handling of the outbreak nevertheless infringe upon individual rights, in particular where privacy is concerned. Using camera surveillance and tracking the cell phone and banking activity of individuals likely infected with coronavirus is grossly in violation of any marginally libertarian principles. But the prevailing point is that with a far softer touch—vastly more respectful toward individual citizens than anywhere else, including our own putative bastion of freedom—the South Korean government has brought about outcomes superior to those of the much heavier handed, authoritarian measures of China, Italy, the U.S., and virtually every other afflicted nation.

TALKING THE TALK AND WALKING THE WALK

Vice Health Minister Kim Gang-Lip summarized the underlying premise of the South Korean government's approach to arresting the spread of the coronavirus: "Without harming the principle of a transparent and open society, we recommend a response system that blends voluntary public participation with creative applications of advanced technology."

While the global spread of the virus is still unfolding and the appearance of new strains may throw the proverbial wrench into Seoul's policy mechanism, at present the results speak for themselves.

Every government action which reduces liberty from any starting point generates net costs, whether put forth under calamitous or idyllic circumstances. Freedom is not a fair-weather proposition. We love it and defend it because it works, in normal times or crisis times.

The quick decision among most countries to deploy their military, force the lockdown of communities, pressure firms to withhold their services, and paralyze individual movement reveals precisely what we suspected but did not fully know about our ruling classes: Our liberties are expendable when they say they are

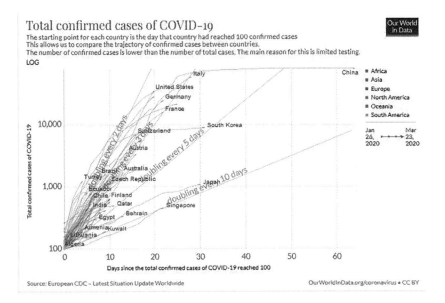

Total confirmed cases of COVID-19

The starting point for each country is the day that country had reached 100 confirmed cases
This allows us to compare the trajectory of confirmed cases between countries.
The number of confirmed cases is lower than the number of total cases. The main reason for this is limited testing.

Source: European CDC – Latest Situation Update Worldwide   OurWorldInData.org/coronavirus • CC BY

CRISIS AND CHAOS

SPECIAL NOTE FROM EDWARD STRINGHAM

March 12, 2020.

These are extremely stressful times for the world economy, particularly financial markets, which have fallen into bear-market territory. The possibility of recession, however temporary, is upon us. Everyone blames the prospect of pandemic disease. That's a correct diagnosis as regards the precipitating factor. But economics and finance are highly complex. Some people think that the markets were due for a correction in any case, and there might be some truth in that.

What's worried me over the last several years is how policy makers are so willing to play so loose with the rule of law, both domestically and internationally. Perhaps it seems that government can get away with slapping 10% or even 25% tariffs on imports, disrupting supply chains around the world and taxing consumers so unnecessarily. It might raise money for the government for a while but it also introduces instability and vulnerabilities.

I could list one thousand other items that make the economy vulnerable: exploding debt, excess regulations, high taxes, tethered banks and financial markets, restrictions on travel, sanctions, wage controls, mandated employment conditions, and so on. Each of these interventions weakens economic structures, often in ways that are not immediately visible.

Something like a pandemic virus can reveal problems that had previously been unseen.

The good news is that this problem will pass in time, but a sound strategy right now, in addition to individual caution, is to free the markets to make the world economy less vulnerable to shocks such as this one.

What we absolutely should not do is make matters worse through massive coercive measures that panic investors, spread public hysteria, and prohibit people from making the best possible choices for their lives. The old truth pertains in normal times as well as in crisis times: people in their own lives are better managers than government-employed authoritarians who bear no liability for the cost of their decisions.

Another way not to deal with this is through further artificial disruption. The Federal Reserve will not save us. Nor will huge spending packages, much less martial law. AIER cannot and will not shrink from explaining these essential truths.

We should remember that the American Institute for Economic Research was founded in the midst of crises. It was 1933. The banks were forcibly closed by central edict. Government demanded that everyone turn in gold to the banks. Then the new chief executive of the US devalued the dollar, voiding millions of contracts and creating chaos. What was the rationale? In Washington, they were just making things up.

Edward Harwood saw the need for calm, serious research, rational decision-making, and truth telling. He was nearly alone in this. His bravery in the face of crisis was singular. It made the difference. Harwood gave the American people an alternative source of analysis at a time when neither government nor academia could be trusted. The government tried to shut him down, not once but three times. He prevailed.

AIER is following that model today in the midst of crisis. Notice how little we are hearing about the Constitution, the Bill of Rights, sound science, and rational action. Most of the loudest voices out there are fueling panic and it is working. Markets are responding accordingly.

Therefore, AIER is providing an alternative with ongoing data reporting and editorials and research that have lifted our website to the largest traffic in our history by far. Our scholars and writers make daily media appearances (you will see more in the next 48 hours).

Everyone at AIER is working extra hours to get the word out about the importance of markets and essential human rights, while maintaining an objective stance without an ideological agenda. Our goal is to be a trustworthy source of information and analysis in times when others are panicking.

Consider the pieces we've posted in the last days (some of which have been read on air by famous commentators who reach tens of millions).

More is forthcoming. Our pledge to you is to continue our work regardless, without fear or favor, with an eye to our mission, and a focus on the task. I've been told over the last several days that important people and institutions on Wall Street and around the country are looking to AIER for leadership.

Times like this force fundamental questions of every institution. In the case of AIER, we are reminded once again why Edward Harwood founded an institution that is among the most valuable in the world today. It will continue to be, in good times and bad.

Sincerely,

Edward Stringham

President, American Institute for Economic Research

GOVERNMENT HAS ONLY ADDED TO INSECURITY AND FEAR
BY JOHN TAMNY

March 14, 2020.

"The only insecurity which is altogether paralyzing to the active energies of producers," wrote John Stuart Mill in *Principles of Political Economy*, "is that arising from the government, or from persons vested with its authority. Against all other depredators there is a hope of defending oneself."

Let's go back to December of 2001 when Enron went bankrupt. Understand what a big deal this was. Not long before it was viewed as the bluest of blue chip companies; one led by some of the smartest people in the world. Roughly eight months later another major American company by the name of Worldcom went under. Yet despite these earthshaking events stock markets were largely sanguine; the DJIA down roughly 3% during the time in question.

It was only *after* the bankruptcies that markets cratered. Translated, Congress and the Bush White House inserted themselves into the situation post-Worldcom with Sarbanes-Oxley. "Sarbox" threatened CEOs with jail if their accounting was incorrect, and President George W. Bush signed the bill into law with great gusto. He enthused to reporters that the legislation was the "toughest anti-corporate crime law since FDR." It was lost on Bush that FDR was not someone to mimic; that he presided over extraordinary economic sluggishness from 1933 to 1939 when, so discredited was his New Deal among Republicans *and* Democrats, that it for all intents and purposes ended.

Needless to say, markets corrected not in response to the bankruptcy of two prominent companies in 2001 and 2002, but in response to the federal government's *reaction* to the bankruptcies. Governments always create solutions worse than the problem. Saddest is that Republicans keep learning this obvious lesson *after* the fact. In case readers have forgotten, the same President Bush decided in 2008 that the "market is not functioning properly" on the way to his Administration fanning the flames of a "crisis" that had little to do with finance, and everything to do with government intervention in the natural workings of an economy on the mend.

It's too easily forgotten that economies are just individuals, and recessions signal individual improvement taking place as those individuals correct bad habits, migrate to work more suited to them, and replenish their finances through more saving.

Economists naively focus on spending as the driver of prosperity, but is the economy of any individual improved by endless waste? Obviously not. Endless, gluttonous consumption is bad for the individual, and it's bad for the economy in total. When individuals are prodigal, capital availability for businesses shrinks. Capital availability for businesses grows as individuals improve their own economic situations by saving. Individual spending caution amid downturns essentially sets the stage for rising growth in the future.

Fast forward to today, a virus that revealed itself in China first led to a pullback in economic activity there. Given the global cooperation involved in all production, this pullback was logically going to weigh on economic activity stateside. But in a normal world free of government meddling, the slowdown would have been self-correcting for the reasons described above. Slower growth would lead to more individual prudence, and subsequently greater capital availability for businesses. The problem was that in a repeat of history, governments around the world stepped on the free part.

The hysterical mayor in Austin, TX, canceled South by Southwest, thus devastating businesses in the city. Cities across the U.S. are declaring states of "emergency" that threaten businesses more broadly. Italy's politicians put parts of the country on lockdown, such that citizens literally need "papers" to get around. In Washington, Republicans who used to know better clamored for the Fed to "slash" interest rates on the naive assumption that governments can magically expand credit availability. They called for "targeted" government spending, travel restrictions, etc.

This has been odd. Republicans are rhetorically skeptical of government action precisely because government spending blunts the laudatory impact of greater private sector capital formation, plus the very notion of government intervention messes with the market's natural direction to the economy's detriment.

Which brings us to President Trump. Though Trump is right that the crisis isn't financial, he somewhat doth protest too much. Markets seem to be saying through equity prices that there *is* a crisis of too much government response to that which many say doesn't pose a major threat, and Trump leads the federal government.

And if coronavirus is a major threat? If so, why has Trump assigned Vice President Pence to the job of orchestrating a response to a health scare? Why didn't he instead make plain in his address on Wednesday night that free markets and free people are always the best solution to problems big and small? He should have, or could have said, "While I think the worry about coronavirus is overstated, assuming it's not, it cannot be stressed enough that the most effective way to fight a threatening illness is for private, profit-motivated markets to match capital with creative, profit-motivated people. We don't go to government for our day-to-day needs, so why on earth would we rely on government during what some say is a crisis?"

Republicans talk a good game about the genius of markets, but any time they don't like the *message* of the markets (see Enron, Worldcom, 2008, and now) they rush to aggressively empower the federal government to intervene. And every time they make things worse than they were before. By definition. It's not a Republican or Democrat thing, it's a free market thing. Markets bring harmony; politicians and governments destabilize.

Some will surely respond that Trump and those around him are privy to information and threats that we're not, thus their meddling, to which the only reasonable reply is "Please be serious." Coronavirus was in the news for weeks without any market correction, only for global politicians to begin inserting themselves into the process. Cascading markets ensued. Well, of course. Indeed, especially if the virus's spread represents a huge global health challenge, that's the surest reason to keep information-deficient governments out of the solution. A Republican administration led by Trump should be making a global case for the rule of the marketplace over the rule of fallible politicians.

The above truth is something Republicans articulate well during the good times. Government is the problem, not the solution. "The scariest words in the English language are I'm from the government, and I'm here to help." But when things get bad? Republicans seemingly forget all that they believe only to substitute their limited knowledge for that of the market. The results are predictable.

About all this, let's be clear that no sane person presumes to know the full truth about the coronavirus. At the same time, the faintly reasonable among us understand that if central planning doesn't work in good times, it most certainly doesn't work in the bad. Too bad Republicans don't grasp this basic truth when understanding it is most crucial. That they don't means that history will rate their cool under pressure as rather sub-standard.

For now, let's make no mistake about what's happening: this is a *political* crisis that investors are putting a crashing market price on. Like all before it. The only insecurity is government.

CELEBRATE THE HEROES WHO STAY OPEN
BY JEFFREY TUCKER

March 14, 2020.

I'm writing on the first Saturday of the Coronapocalpyse. I just returned from a shopping trip in town.

The laundromat and dry cleaners are open. The UPS store is open. Target, Marshalls, McDonald's, and the hardware stores are open. The farmers' market is selling pies. Dunkin' Donuts is doing a brisk business in coffee and the usual fare. CVS is welcoming all.

All grocery stores are open. But for the empty shelves that usually hold toilet paper, everything else is stocked up. Veggies. Meat. Milk. Soups. Cosmetics. Trucks are arriving to restock shelves after brisk sales of just about everything.

Automotive places are changing oil, repairing issues, and taking new customers. Antique malls are hocking wares. Coffee shops are serving lattes and muffins. Restaurants have lunch and drinks. Clothing stores are holding special sales on winter clothing as they always do this time of year. Gas stations are doing business. People are driving around, walking around, greeting each other in a friendly way, smiling at each other.

It's normalcy all around, which is important because if you had only been holed up in your home and watching TV, you might believe that the world outside is in total pandemonium. It seems like many people are pushing for that or even think complete panic is justified. Instead what we are seeing is a sense of calm caution. Social distance. No handshakes. Big smiles instead. Lines at sinks in public bathrooms where people are washing hands. Hand sanitizer is everywhere.

Otherwise, there is calm. No one is freaking out. The shelves are stocked up so you don't see hoarding.

I'm grateful for all of this. The people who make this possible are heroes. They are probably preventing pandamonium. So long as people feel that essential needs can be met, they maintain civility and morality (which is always a casualty in panics), giving us all a much greater chance of getting through this.

And while we are passing out blessings, save one for Domino's Pizza. This is how you innovate.

WE'RE HERE TO DELIVER, HOWEVER YOU WANT IT!

Here at Domino's, we're the food delivery experts. Whether you prefer a delivery handed to you at your door, left at a reception desk, or a 'contactless' delivery where your store's delivery expert will leave your order safely at your front door, the Delivery Instructions box is the place to request any special directions you have for your store. At the end of the day we want you to enjoy a hot and delicious meal, regardless of how you want it delivered.

More about 'contactless' delivery:

It would be so easy to join the "shut down everything" chorus that you see online. How grossly irresponsible such demands are! In any case, most businesses are okay refusing to do so. And so far as I can tell, all the employees and certainly the customers in these places are happy for the opportunity to serve. And serve they do: enterprise is performing an amazing public service right now, and getting no praise for it in the media, so far as I can see.

You say: but they are all profiting from pandemic disease! I say: I hope so. They should all be justly rewarded for their service.

Also, while millions of people are extremely worried about losing their jobs, the people working today have an assurance that their businesses can continue to meet payroll because they are doing commerce. People are talking about survival right now but having a job and keeping the income flowing is also surviving.

Of course you could say all these activities are low risk because they involve only small gatherings, whereas many places have banned gatherings over a certain size (how that is Constitutional is another question). But in the United Kingdom, they have gone the extra step of maintaining calm by not banning sports events, concerts, and the like.

The Wall Street Journal reports:[109]

> Britain isn't alone in taking a more restrained approach. The Canadian government has also held off banning mass gatherings, although several of the country's provinces have announced their own tougher measures. Germany is also proving far less interventionist than other European nations.

I don't know what should and shouldn't be shut down. But neither does the government have some special magical access to information on risk probabilities and the proper way forward. In fact, government is the last institution that should be making this judgment. Government acts out of self-interest; enterprise acts in the public interest. The obvious answer here is to leave the decision to private actors who are in the best position to make a good judgment on what should shut and what should open.

---

109 Colchester, Max. 2020. "U.K. Looks to Slow Coronavirus By a Different, Albeit Controversial, Way." *The Wall Street Journal*, March 14.

I do know that the more commercial life can continue as cautionary normalcy, the more we'll all be in a position to get through this. The less economic damage is done. The more people keep their jobs. The less human suffering there will be.

The way to make an emergency worse is to shutter the shops and jettison commercial transactions of the goods and services we depend on for the good life and for survival itself. Commerce is society's lifeblood. Nothing is gained from forcibly cutting it off.

In normal times, we take all of this for granted. We pick up meat and veggies from the store without a thought. We buy medicines and health aids routinely without consciousness that these things don't have to exist. We go to the hardware store as if it were a chore, something we must do to repair the sink and get lightbulbs.

Take it all away and then we will see what the real apocalypse looks like. We would take an unnerving and scary pandemic and turn it into complete social collapse. This is a reality that none of us have ever faced and, god willing, we never will. And we won't so long as we leave it to the discretion of commercial establishments and consumers to make their own choices. Take away that freedom and all we are left with is the barbarism of material deprivation and poverty.

And so I smiled and said thank you to every employee stocking shelves, running the cash registers, mailing my packages, taking my dry cleaning, and selling me bleach wipes. Blessed are those who eschew the crazy demand to "shut down everything" and instead continue to serve the people.

THOSE SHELVES WOULDN'T BE EMPTY IF WE HADN'T STOPPED "CAPITALISM"

BY ART CARDEN

March 15, 2020.

You've seen the pictures on your social media feeds: Empty shelves across America. Panic-buying. Hoarding. You might have even seen comments from self-described socialists saying, "Here's what the US looks like under capitalism in a crisis" and perhaps mocking people who point to regularly empty store shelves in Venezuela as a condemnation of socialism. There are two problems with this, though.

First, this is a temporary phenomenon brought on by a sudden panic. Shelves emptied by panic buyers are rare in free market economies and frequent in alleged workers' paradises.

Second, and importantly, this is *exactly what the supply-and-demand model we teach in introductory economics courses predicts when we actively prevent the free market from functioning.* The shelves aren't empty because of free-market capitalism. They're empty because of active interference with free-market capitalism. Specifically, governments aren't letting prices change to reflect new market conditions.

States are declaring states of emergency, perhaps rightly so in light of some of the risks we likely face as COVID-19 spreads. Bundled with sensible emergency measures like recommendations about social distancing, touching others, and so on are price controls as politicians rattle their sabers about "price gouging" and "profiteering."

These are basically embargoes on knowledge.[110] Higher prices serve a crucial social role by asking people to think a little harder about whether or not they really *need* that much hand sanitizer or toilet paper or whether they might be able to get by with a little less. The unintended consequence? There's a roll of toilet paper or a bottle of hand sanitizer waiting for the next person who wants it at the market price.

This gets turned upside-down when we go after so-called "price gougers." Grotesquely, they get tarred as villains while it's actually the politicians who are making the problem worse by interfering with prices. They are outraged that prices are rising in the face of high demand and uncertain future supply, but that's exactly what prices should do under these circumstances.

A lot of this stems from a fundamental confusion about cost. Critics and activists think that someone is selling unacceptably "above cost" and reaping an illegitimate windfall profit when they charge a price that is a lot higher than what they paid for the product from a wholesaler plus a "reasonable" profit.

This gets cost all wrong, though. At the point of sale, the cost of selling a roll of toilet paper is not what the retailer paid the wholesaler. That's irrelevant to current market conditions. The cost of selling a roll of toilet paper to *you* is what the person behind you in line would have paid. Suppose you're willing to pay $2 while the person behind you is willing to pay $5. *Everyone* is going through a hard time right now; it's not exactly clear why the person behind the counter and the person behind you should give up their gains from trade for you.

---

110 Carden, Art. 2019. "Price Gouging Laws Are Knowledge Embargoes That Should Be Repealed." *Forbes*, August 31.

At this point, people might be objecting, "But demand is a reflection of willingness *and ability to pay*, so it might be unfair to the poor." This makes intuitive sense, but I think there's a serious complication with the "ability to pay" qualification: namely, if you are fortunate enough to spend your last $2 on a roll of toilet paper for which the person behind you is willing to pay $5, then you are actually sacrificing not $2 for the roll of toilet paper, but $5. You're "paying," albeit implicitly, by *not* selling the toilet paper for $5—and you are, therefore, demonstrating an "ability to pay" of $5.

This is similar to an example I'm fond of using when I teach about opportunity costs. Think about tickets to sporting events. Suppose tickets to the Big Game are going for $500 each. By sheer luck, you find a ticket on the ground. Does this mean you now get to go to the game for "free?"

No. Going to the game still costs you $500 (plus the opportunity cost of your time). You could have sold the ticket for $500, but you chose to go to the game. Fundamentally, there's no difference between finding $500 on the ground and buying a ticket with it and finding a ticket on the ground that you could sell for $500.

Hence, I'm skeptical of "ability to pay" as an objection to high prices during disasters unless transaction costs are really high—and even then, I think the solution is to identify and overcome the sources of the transaction costs.

But shouldn't people charge low prices because it's the *right* thing to do? Maybe. People respond to a complex mix of incentives and motivations, and one of the more heartening responses to the COVID-19 outbreak has been the way in which a lot of publishers have opened up their online products for students and instructors suddenly faced with moving their courses online. Benevolence is one motivation among many, though, and the fact remains that we get a lot more hand sanitizer, toilet paper, and other supplies when we make room for people who are just in it for the money.

You may not like their motivations, but they're doing something your state's governor and attorney general aren't doing. Namely, they're getting valuable emergency supplies into your hands. Maybe humanitarian impulses are elegant and more civilized ways of getting goods into the hands of the needy compared to the profit motive, just as a lightsaber might be an elegant and more civilized way of killing an enemy than a blaster. At the end of the day, though, both motivations (just like both weapons) get the job done.

As the economist Yoram Barzel explained in his under-appreciated paper "A Theory of Rationing by Waiting," it's hard to give away money in a way that actually helps the people we want to help.[111] As economists point out whenever price ceilings come up, price ceilings don't reduce what we pay. They change how we pay, with more of the putative benefits of our purchases being consumed by search costs. Someone waiting in a long line for low-priced hand sanitizer and toilet paper is incurring a cost (his valuable time) but not producing a benefit for someone else.

Here's a real-life illustration. Various outlets report that a Tennessee man bought 17,700 bottles of hand sanitizer with a view toward selling them at a markup online. Amazon refuses to do business with him, which is their right as a private firm. However, they would probably expose themselves to multiple price-gouging prosecutions were they to allow him to sell hand sanitizer at a hefty markup via their site.

---

111 Barzel, Yoram. 1974. "A Theory of Rationing by Waiting." *The Journal of Law & Economics*, 17(1): 73-95.

The perverse result is that instead of 17,700 bottles of hand sanitizer at a price of $10 or $20 or even $100, people can, at least in the very short run, get *no hand sanitizer at any price*. The effective price of a bottle of hand sanitizer when there is none to be had, as Michael Munger has pointed out, is effectively infinity.[112]

This is a difficult time for a lot of people, and it's understandable and admirably humane to want to help others in their time of need. We aren't doing them any favors, however, by saying that they won't be allowed to pay very much for a bottle of hand sanitizer they can't get anyway.

---

112 Munger, Michael and Russ Roberts. 2007. "Munger on Price Gouging." *The Library of Economics and Liberty*, EconTalk January 8.

HOW THE US BOTCHED CORONAVIRUS TESTING
BY ADAM THIERER

March 12, 2020.

Many Americans are wondering why public health officials are not doing more to speed up deployment of coronavirus testing kits. What would happen if a private team of doctors offered an effective test before federal regulators approved one?

Dr. Helen Y. Chu and a team of infectious disease experts in Seattle found out the answer: The government will stop you.

According to a *New York Times* investigation, Dr. Chu and a team of researchers in the Seattle area had been collecting nasal swabs from residents experiencing symptoms in an effort to monitor the spread of flu in the region.[113] It turned out they could use their test to monitor the coronavirus outbreak, but they would need approval from state and federal officials to do so legally.

"But nearly everywhere Dr. Chu turned, officials repeatedly rejected the idea," the Times investigation shows, even though it was clear that the virus was already ravaging China and likely to spread in the US. She and her team decided to start performing coronavirus tests without government approval anyway. Their worst fears were confirmed as they were able to document that a local teenager had the virus. Government officials later confirmed the findings from Dr. Chu's team. According to Times reporters Sheri Fink and Mike Baker, however, regulators

---

113 Fink, Sheri and Mike Baker. 2020. "'It's Just Everywhere Already': How Delays in Testing Set Back the U.S. Coronavirus Response." *The New York Times*, March 10.

still would not allow her team to move forward with more testing:

> Federal and state officials said the flu study could not be repurposed because it did not have explicit permission from research subjects; the labs were also not certified for clinical work. While acknowledging the ethical questions, Dr. Chu and others argued there should be more flexibility in an emergency during which so many lives could be lost. On Monday night, state regulators told them to stop testing altogether.

Fink and Baker note that the government's failure to allow this study to go forward, "was just one in a series of missed chances by the federal government to ensure more widespread testing during the early days of the outbreak, when containment would have been easier." Sadly, matters are not improving. "The continued delays [in getting government-approved testing kits] have made it impossible for officials to get a true picture of the scale of the growing outbreak," the reporters note. Meanwhile, early government-approved diagnostic tests were contaminated, meaning the Seattle test should have been welcomed as an alternative.[114] The journalists conclude that:

> The Seattle Flu Study illustrates how existing regulations and red tape—sometimes designed to protect privacy and health— have impeded the rapid rollout of testing nationally, while other countries ramped up much earlier and faster. Faced with a public health emergency on a scale potentially not seen in a century,

---

114 Lim, David, Sarah Karlin-Smith and Dan Diamond. 2020. "U.S. health officials probe coronavirus test problems at CDC." *Politico*, March 1.

the United States has not responded nimbly.

Needless to say, this is a public health catastrophe in the making. Overly precautionary regulations may have undermined public health and cost lives.[115]

RED TAPE VS. PUBLIC HEALTH

Officials at the Centers for Disease Control and Prevention and the Good and Drug Administration say they are working aggressively to come up with better testing procedures to counter the virus, which has now been classified as a pandemic by the World Health Organization.[116] Even if it is true that federal officials are trying their hardest to speed up testing, the government's rejection of the Seattle Flu Study testing effort represents a disturbing example of the failure of good intentions in action.[117] Just because precautionary-minded regulators *say* they have our best interests in mind, it does not necessarily mean their policies *actually* serve the public good.

In this case, highly restrictive procedures for virus testing have had the unintended consequence of shutting down tests that could detect outbreaks and save lives. Going by the book apparently mattered more than getting good results. "This virus is faster than the FDA," a University of Washington Medical Center doctor told the *Times*.

---

115 Thierer, Adam. 2019. "How Many Lives Are Lost Due to the Precautionary Principle?" *The Bridge*, October 31.

116 Chappell, Bill. 2020. "Coronavirus: COVID-19 Is Now Officially A Pandemic, WHO Says." *NPR*, March 11.

117 O'Sullivan, Andrea and Adam Thierer. 2019. "Tech Policy, Unintended Consequences & the Failure of Good Intentions." *The Bridge*, September 25.

Incredibly, that doctor also said that at one point the agency was asking him to submit materials through the mail in addition to over email. Strict regulatory paperwork procedures have triumphed over common sense.

Incidentally, the Seattle Flu Study team is funded by the Bill & Melinda Gates Foundation, and health officials from the Foundation and from the state of Washington petitioned the CDC to consider using the Seattle team's test results. The CDC simply punted on the issue and told them to seek FDA approval. The Seattle Flu Study did not strictly comply with established CDC and FDA lab regulations, however, and so the answer from federal regulators always came back the same: No. "We felt like we were sitting, waiting for the pandemic to emerge," Dr. Chu told the *Times*. "We could help. We couldn't do anything."

THE ETHICS OF EVASION

However, what is most interesting about this example of innovation-limiting regulation is that it did not stop Dr. Chu and her team from moving forward, at least not initially. Instead, they engaged in what we might think of as "evasive entrepreneurialism" or "technological civil disobedience." They went ahead and tested for the coronavirus without permission to prove that they might be able to help. Stated differently, they broke the law in pursuit of a higher goal.

What are we to make of the ethics of that decision? It is a thorny question and one that I discuss in a forthcoming book, which documents the rise of evasive entrepreneurialism and technological civil disobedience in many different contexts.[118] Evasive entrepreneurs are

---

118 Thierer, Adam. 2018. "Evasive Entrepreneurialism and Technological Civil Disobedience: Basic Definitions." *The Bridge*, July 20.

innovators who do not always conform to social or legal norms. They take advantage of new devices, platforms, and methods of production to experiment with new ways of doing things. Sometimes they do so intentionally to evade laws or regulations they find offensive, confusing, or counter-productive. That's why I refer to it as technological civil disobedience.

Dr. Chu's evasive act of testing-without-approval tees up the core ethical and legal question raised repeatedly in my new book: Why is it that many people often justify acts of evasive entrepreneurialism after the fact, but few defend them as they are happening? Stated differently, why are people (including *The New York Times* of all papers) cheering on Dr. Helen Chu and her team right now instead of suggesting they be fined or sent to jail? After all, technically speaking, they broke the law. Some will say she and her team can be forgiven because their evasive actions could help save lives and, therefore, the ends justified the means. But who would have stood by her and her team when they initially set out to innovate around the system to achieve that result?

The answer in this and many other instances is not black-and-white. But evasive innovation could clearly help save lives in this case, which must have some bearing on the moral calculus here.

PUTTING THE GENIE BACK IN THE BOTTLE

But let's consider the case against evasive entrepreneurialism in this context. To be sure, the ethics of medical testing are extraordinarily complicated. At the individual level, there are serious concerns about patient medical privacy. In the aggregate, there are legitimate questions about what types of tests can be trusted as well as concerns about mistaken results fueling panics or misguided treatments.

But even putting those ethical questions aside, this case raises a more practical reality: New technological capabilities—in the medical space and others—are becoming more decentralized and democratized.

In the old days, "doing science" was exclusively the domain of experts in big institutions. Going by the book was more straightforward in that environment. Things get more complicated once the genie is out of the bottle and more institutions and individuals have access to technologies that allow more decentralized forms of trial-and-error experimentation.

Risk-averse regulators and their highly precautionary mountains of red tape can only stand in the way of so much of this. Policymakers will need a new approach for technological governance in this new world. Flexibility and humility will be essential. Regulators should not throw out the old rulebooks altogether, of course. Some precautionary procedures still make sense. Not everyone should be running their own lab or doing their own tests. Permissionless innovation has its limits.

On the other hand, lawmakers and regulators could borrow a page from the permissionless innovation playbook and allow more experimental trials, flexible testing procedures, targeted waivers, and *ex post* regulatory reviews as opposed to *ex ante* regulatory prohibitions on any and all innovations.

Evasive entrepreneurialism should be thought of as an important part of a broader discovery process that appreciates the profound importance of ongoing, decentralized trial-and-error experimentation to the process of social learning. Lawmakers should find a way to accommodate a little more outside-the-box thinking and innovating, especially when our lives are on the line.

TO KILL MARKETS IS THE WORST POSSIBLE PLAN
BY RICHARD M. EBELING

March 16, 2020.

Momentous events usually leave strong memories on those who have lived through them, and those memories often become passed on to later generations in the form of historical interpretations of why and what had happened in the past. This has certainly been so in the cases of the Great Depression, the Second World War, the Civil Rights Movement, the Vietnam War, the terrorist attack of September 11, 2001, the financial crisis of 2008-2009, and now, no doubt, in the face of the Coronavirus pandemic of 2020.

One very important aspect to many of the interpretations of these past events is the lessons drawn in terms of the role of government in the free society. The dust is very far from settling in this latest health crisis that is, truly, enveloping the world. But even in the urgency of finding and implementing ways of minimizing the impact on human life and well-being from the Coronavirus, the outlines of how this crisis may be interpreted in the future is already showing its outline in the present.

WRONG LESSONS THAT MAY BE LEARNED FROM THE CORONAVIRUS CRISIS
One lesson that will, no doubt, be claimed is that this has once again demonstrated the limits of free markets and the need for activist and centralized governmental oversight, control and command. Dealing with a health issue like the Coronavirus cannot be left up to the decisions or discretion of individuals or even local governments. There has to be designed and directed health-management through central planning by government "experts" and agencies in this type of crisis,

it will be said.

As part of this lesson will be the additional claim, as happened in many previous national disasters, of the need to prevent the greed of those in the private sector who try to take personal advantage of a human disaster by "price gouging" and grasping at unwarranted profits at their neighbor's expense. Price controls in the form of price ceilings and possibly government-organized rationing of essential goods in short supply must be placed outside the everyday arena of ordinary market supply and demand, it will be insisted.

A second lesson that will be suggested by some will be the "dangers" and undesirability of international interdependency for many of the goods and services needed by communities and countries, the supplies of which can become limited or completely lost during a world health crisis such as the Coronavirus due to the supply chains of production that criss-cross national boundaries under the current global system of division of labor.

Better that some essential and vital resource supplies and manufacturing of such goods be "homespun;" that is, produced and supplied domestically in the name of the "national interest." Some conservatives who have long been wary of "American" industries and employment being "lost" to producers and workers abroad are already saying that the current health crisis shows the need for greater economic self-sufficient "independence."

And, third, voices are being heard along a wide range of the political and ideological spectrum for the need and necessity for "activist" fiscal and monetary policies to temper and stabilize the negative financial, production, and employment recession-like effects that the Coronavirus is spreading around the world. Markets cannot be left on their own without even more dire consequences for societies beyond the tragic physical hardships and losses to human life from the pandemic.

It is said that even lower interest rates and greater amounts of money and credit are needed to bolster investment and production, while fiscal "ease" in the form of government spending and general or targeted tax breaks are essential to keep small, medium and too-big-to-fail larger businesses afloat. Investment stimulus and aggregate demand-management are once again shown to be the tried and true Keynesian spending cures to the economic ills of society, by the macroeconomic policy managers.

GOVERNMENT FAILURES IN CHINA AND AMERICA IN FIGHTING THE VIRUS
Given these likely and emerging interpretations of the coronavirus pandemic, it is, first of all, important to appreciate that delays in effective communication about the existence and potential dangers from the virus, and then the failure of more widely spread testing in the United States are, in fact, failures not of a free marketplace but of government central planning and control.

The press has been full of stories of how early indications about the virus and its potential dangers were suppressed by the Chinese communist government. The reality of this went "viral" even on China's highly censored and controlled social media platforms when news got out that one of the physicians attempting to inform and publicize what was being discovered was ordered by the Chinese government to keep quiet, and then ended up dying from the Coronavirus himself.

And in typical political form, the Chinese government has attempted to shield President Xi Jinping from any criticism of being responsible for policies that delayed an earlier response by making up factitious stories about how President Xi was "ahead of the curve," guiding and directing the nationwide lockdown and medical commands that have "saved" the country. And that it was really all due to the U.S. military whose personnel visiting the epicenter city of Wuhan brought the virus to China to keep that proud nation "in its place," in a world of American "hegemony."

The media in America, including "The New York Times," have chronicled how America's own health care central planning system prevented many of the more early responses to the virus due to the rigid top-down rules and procedures imposed by the Pure Food and Drug Administration (FDA) and the Centers for Disease Control (CDC) in hamstringing local and decentralized development and use of Coronavirus testing tools, since nothing could be done without approval and permission of the American government's health and drug planners.

Furthermore, when some "rogue" healthcare providers around the country attempted to disobey the health care overseers and social engineers by utilizing their own testing methods and equipment to determine who and to what extent the virus may have spread in their area of the U.S., they were told to cease and desist, and wait for whatever and whenever the testing devices were made available to them by and according to the standards of the federal regulators. (See Adam Thierer's article, "How the US Botched Coronavirus Testing".)[119]

However, rather than questioning the centralized process of permitting the development and use of methods for disease testing, the lesson to be learned, it is presumed, is that the government merely needs to introduce more "flexible" rules and procedures to better team up with state and local health and medical treatment agencies to deal with the current and future crises of this type.

---

119 See article herein entitled "How the US Botched Coronavirus Testing."

GOVERNMENT REGULATION VS. MARKET DISCOVERY

The idea that virtually all such matters might better be left up to the private, competitive marketplace seems to not even be considered in the arena of debate. Potential "market failures" are seen everywhere, and possible "government failures" are brushed aside as incidental errors and omissions on the pathway to better political oversight of health and medicine.

But as Austrian economist Friedrich A. Hayek (1899-1992) argued more than half a century ago, "Competition is a Discovery Procedure" (1969) through which individuals and enterprises have the opportunity and the incentives to not only discover the new and better and improved, but to find out what might be possible. Not only can we not know until a competitive process has been allowed to play out who may be the "winner," but it is only in an arena of competition that individuals have the motive and ability to find out what they are capable of; something that they, themselves, cannot fully know the answer to until they are at liberty to try and have a reason to want to.

The hoops and hurdles that pharmaceutical companies and other manufacturers of medical and health related products must make their way through under the rules, procedures and permissions of federal agencies such as the FDA and the CDC only succeed in reducing the incentives, raising the costs, and narrowing the field of those who otherwise might be willing and able to undertake research, experimentation and marketing of those medicines and medical-related products that could save or improve lives.

A common and reasonable response is, of course, but what about standards and experimental procedures to assure consumer safety from poorly tested and hastily marketed health-related products in the pursuit of profit? Is that not the reasonable rationale for government to centrally approve and oversee regulatory methods over all such marketed products?

THE INCENTIVES OF SELF-REGULATING MARKETS

The word "regulate" is defined by Webster's dictionary as meaning "to govern or direct according to rule," or "to bring order, method, or uniformity to..." The Oxford Dictionary says to, "control (something, especially a business activity) by means of rules and regulations." Understood in this way, there is little if anything that any of us do that is not according to "regulation," both as individuals and in association with others, even without government.

We each have our time schedules and procedures that we follow in various ways and to varying detail. Even when what a person does does not seem to make much sense, do we not sometimes say such things as, just look beneath the surface and you'll "discover the method to the madness?" Private sector clubs, associations, business enterprises and arenas of market interaction all have their own participant-generated regulations to facilitate and coordinate how and for what the participants interact with each other for smoother and more predictable pathways to mutual success; and to reinforce confidence on the part of any participant about how his interlocutor has acted and what procedures they may have followed leading up to the transaction and trade.

Many of those rules and procedures that "regularize" how people do things, for whatever purposes, and with whatever degree of surety of reliability and confidence in the conduct of those with whom we buy and sell have, historically, emerged before the modern era of government regulation, and often continues parallel to or independently of any such regulatory rules and procedure imposed by government.

No pharmaceutical or medical equipment company concerned with its long-term viability as a profit-making enterprise can count on staying the course in the marketplace by killing their customers, adulterating their products, or making intentional false promises or guarantees. Hollywood movies may make their millions by portraying every drug company as a murderous monster in its pursuit of more profitable market shares, but that is not how real, market-based companies can afford to operate. Possible lawsuits, sky-high insurance premiums and the loss of brand-name reputation always dog any company thinking of cutting corners to any extent. (See my review of "Regulation Without the State".)[120]

REGULATIONS SERVING VESTED INTERESTS

Economists have long emphasized what is sometimes called the "capture" theory of government regulation. That is, the industry being regulated by the government often has lobbied for that political intervention, or when this is not the case, has come to see it as an opportunity to use the regulatory intervention as means of raising the "barriers to entry" to any would-be new entrants and enterprises that might want to compete against the existing and established firms in that corner of the market.

Therefore, one of the central purposes of leaving markets free of government control is precisely to not block the way to potential rivals and to force the current firms in that industry to more effectively compete and innovate to maintain any profitable position in the market; and to permit the flexibility and adaptability to changing market conditions. It is open competition that assures consumer-oriented

---

120 Ebeling, Richard M. 2001. "Book Review: Regulation without the State." *The Future of Freedom Foundation*, June 1.

production and pricing, and it is government regulation that tends to foster rules and restrictions designed to shelter existing firms from new and creative competition.

If any such firms may be clothed with a "black hat," it is those who wish to use the government's regulatory power to, therefore, stymy market competition. The fault is not with a free market, but from the introduction of government interventions and regulatory agencies manned by those who presume to know what is better for people than those people themselves, and whose activities almost inescapably always fall victim to the designs of the larger companies those agencies are set up to regulate.

In addition, sight should not be lost of the self-interested purposes of those who live on and off government agencies such as the FDA and the CDC. Their recent responses to attempts to introduce methods and procedures outside of their straitjacket of regulatory control demonstrates their desire not to permit the weakening of the institutional structures by which they justify their power, positions, and incomes within the government maze of bureaucracies.

PRICE CONTROLS ONLY MAKE SUPPLY SITUATIONS WORSE

The other ingredient in the regulatory mix is that when a crisis occurs such as the latest one in the form of the Coronavirus, concerns and even "panic" break out among many people in an attempt to obtain supplies of those goods viewed as essential or desirable to meet the real and imagined circumstances now facing them in the impacted communities. Around the United States, most recently, fears of mandated lockdowns and voluntary quarantining to reduce spreading of the Coronavirus may reduce or stop the availability of such essential products as toilet paper or bacterial and virus-reducing cleaning products.

Retail store shelves normally filled with such products are either empty or low in inventory. People have been scurrying from store to store in search of any brand name and type of toilet paper, for instance, even if they are not sure whether it might not "rub them the wrong way!" In the face of normal production levels and shipment schedules, quantities in the supply line to the retail stores have been lacking due to the unusual and unexpected increase in immediate demand.

To prevent "price gouging" 34 states currently have laws on the books making it illegal to "excessively" increase prices on high demand goods during a declared or generally considered "emergency." This is meant to prevent those selling these products from "unfairly" taking advantage of people needing and wanting such products.

After forty centuries of price controls, it would be hoped that, finally, the counterproductive and disastrous effects of all such systems of government-imposed price controls would have been learned by now.[121] But, alas, not. Market prices have work to do, including in times of social crises such as the one with the Coronavirus. But the government price controllers seem to never learn.

Price flexibility enables the coordination and balancing of market supplies and demands at moments in time and across time, given the degree of demand for goods and the existing supplies of them in the same time frames. Market-generated prices create the incentives for consumers to economize in the face of increased demands or reduced supply, and they create incentives for sellers to find ways to increase production and availability when there is a decrease in existing supply or an increase in consumer demands to buy.

---

121 Schuettinger, Robert L. & Eamonn F. Butler. *Forty Centuries of Wage and Price Controls: How Not to Fight Inflation.* The Heritage Foundation: Washington D.C. Caroline House, Publishers, Inc.

PRICES CONVEY KNOWLEDGE AND COORDINATE MARKETS

As F. A. Hayek also emphasized, all of the knowledge in society exists in no one place or in any one mind or group of minds, no matter how knowledgeable and well-informed those individuals may consider themselves to be. Knowledge, in its many facets and forms, is dispersed and decentralized among all the minds of all the people in society in their, respective, corners of the world.

The "social problem," Hayek argued, is to have some means and method to bring to bear what others know that can serve the purposes and needs we may have in mind when we are inescapably separated from each other by time and space. That is the communication role of a competitive and unrestricted price system. People in different parts of the country or the globe are able to inform each other about what they want or what they can supply through the medium of market prices. It is like a shorthand or Morse Code of supplying to others the relevant minimum of information about what and where and at what value people somewhere want and would be willing to buy what those others might have available or could produce to fill the demand.

While the concern has recently been expressed about the general availability of Coronavirus testing kits, effective face masks, respiratory equipment, and related medical supplies, the fact is that there are different intensities of demand for them, given where the higher clusters of reported or feared cases of infected people are located around the country. Allowing the price system to openly and competitively function, with no government rationing scheme preventing or delaying supply-shifting from less to more urgent areas, would rapidly assure that the existing supplies of these things are more efficiently and effectively reallocated to where prices indicate they are most in demand to meet the medical needs for them.

But not only would a functioning price system for these and other goods bring about a more "rational" allocation of the scarce and given quantities of these goods in the present, but rising and unrestrained prices for the various goods, with no penalty for profits earned from their current and future sale, would also serve as the essential method and mechanism to generate the incentives to increase their supplies over time and work to improve their effectiveness in fighting the virus. That is part of the advantage, dare I say, beauty, of setting creative minds free with the liberty to reap the benefits from applying their talents to solve a social problem like the current one.

The Coronavirus crisis has been compared to the seriousness of war against a life-threatening enemy. It is perhaps interesting to note that in September 1939, as Great Britain just entered into its war against Nazi Germany and the British economy needed to gear up for the conflict through new patterns for using resources and goods away from civilian uses to military production, Hayek wrote an article making the case for leaving market prices free from government controls:

> The required quantities of the urgently needed factors of pro-
> duction ought to be released from those uses in which they can
> be dispensed with at the least sacrifice of other necessary things.
> But this is just what will happen if the scarce factor rises in
> price, since producers will dispense with it precisely for those
> purposes where it costs least to do without it... A little con-
> sideration will show that a rise in price is incomparably more
> efficient a method of bringing forth the additional supplies than
> alternative methods of achieving the same result [through price
> controls and rationing].

Price controls only succeed in short-circuiting the means of people to converse and communicate with each other so they can share vital information in the simplest and most adaptable form to constantly and continuously bring about the short-term and longer-term adjustments of goods and resources to meet the needs of people, including at a moment of a crisis like the present one. (See my article, "Price Controls Attack the Freedom of Speech.")[122]

USING THE CORONAVIRUS AS A RATIONALE FOR ECONOMIC NATIONALISM

The Coronavirus crisis began in China, and the world soon saw the Chinese government's draconian locking down and shutting in of areas of the country containing tens of millions of people in the attempt to stop or slow down the spread of the virus. The supply chains of raw materials, component parts, and manufacturing and product assembly that interdependently link China with the economies of many other countries around the world were suddenly disrupted and thrown into disarray.

Companies in countries not yet significantly affected by the Coronavirus searched around for possible substitute supplies and warned of the unavailability of various goods due to the production stoppages in the Chinese stages of numerous production processes.

In this setting, voices are being heard calling for a turn to greater economic nationalism, with government limiting a continuing dependency on, for instance, the Chinese market. For example, conservative writer Patrick Buchanan said in his March 13 column: "In retrospect, was it wise to have relied on China to produce essential parts for the supply chains of goods vital to our national security? Does

---

122 Ebeling, Richard M. 2019. "Price Controls Attack the Freedom of Speech." *American Institute for Economic Research*, September 17.

it appear wise to have moved the production of pharmaceuticals and lifesaving drugs for heart disease, strokes and diabetes to China?"[123]

The implication being that the U.S. government should manipulate the market through taxes, protectionism, and regulations to bring production of these goods back to America.

Economic nationalists like Buchanan seem to be applying Rahm Emanuel's now famous phrase of never letting a serious crisis go to waste in the service of a political agenda that might be harder to push in calmer social and economic times. Supply chain stoppages and shortages that could and would easily be reversed once the virus finishes running its course, and if governments kept out of the way and allowed production relationships between companies and countries to restore and rebalance themselves, are being used as rationales for restricting a market-based global network of specialization and division of labor.

THE BENEFITS FROM TRADE AND TEMPORARY DISRUPTIONS

People trade because each participant finds that he is able to obtain from someone else a good or service that would cost them more to obtain in terms of used resources, labor, or time if made through their own efforts. If I can buy something that I desire from my neighbor for, say, $10 when if I tried to make it myself it would cost me $15 in resources, time and labor, I am far better off acquiring it from that neighbor, and having $5 left over in my pocket to spend on other things I otherwise could not have afforded.

---

123 Buchanan, Patrick J. 2020. "Will the Coronavirus Kill the New World Order?" *Patrick J Buchanan*, March 13.

My neighbor, in turn, sells me his product for that $10 because the $10 that he earns enables him to buy something he desires that would cost him more than the $10 if he were to try to make that product for himself. Each of us gets a bargain; we each get what we want from the other at better terms (lower costs) than if we attempted to do so through autarky; that is, economic self-sufficiency, in some or all the things we might otherwise be able to obtain in exchange from trading partners, whether next door or halfway around the world.

A wide variety of political criticisms may easily be made against the communist government in China in terms of both its domestic and foreign policies, and a proponent of a free-market liberal society could easily make that into a very long list. But the coronavirus fits more in the category of a natural disaster, like an earthquake or a hurricane, that disrupts and destroys lives and property, and reduces economic potentials and possibilities for a period of time.

Again, assuming no undue government interventions getting in the way, the human beings whose actions are behind all the work, savings and investment in society, usually undertake the needed reconstruction and rebuilding within a reasonable period of time, after which "life goes on as before."

Tragically, several thousands of lives have been, and many more may be lost before the coronavirus runs its course around the world. And in the meantime, production processes are—and will be—slowed down or temporarily halted. But factory buildings have not collapsed, farmlands have not been swallowed up by the earth, great fires have not destroyed places where people live, and cities still stand just as they did before the virus started making people ill.

In other words, "this too will pass," and people will go back to work, get back to eating out at restaurants, shopping at their favorite stores, and planning their next vacations at home and abroad. While many in society are experiencing a high degree of anxiety and panic due to the uncertainties surrounding some of the properties of this virus, and while the mass media and governments have helped fuel those fears, the fact is that this virus is just a "cousin" of the serious flus that strike humanity around the globe with almost clockwork annual regularity, and which, unfortunately, take tens of thousands of lives each time.

If a hurricane or a drought wipes out the orange harvest in Florida, we would consider it foolish if the people and government of Alaska decided that it would now be wise to invest in hothouses to have orange "independence" at home due to the uncertainties of Florida weather. Wholesalers and retailers in Alaska search out temporary substitute suppliers of oranges located somewhere else in the world, and then return to buying oranges from Florida next season, if once more Florida farmers offer the better fruit at the more attractive price.

A very bad lesson, therefore, from the coronavirus episode would be to in any way suggest that the disruptions caused by it to the supply chains of international trade justify severing through deliberate government policy the near universal benefits that all of us everywhere on the planet gain from participating in the worldwide system of division of labor, which now includes China. The citizens of any country whose government attempted to do so would experience losses in their qualities and standards of living that have been and could be theirs only through the collaborative global interdependencies of market-oriented specialization and trade.

A DIARRHEA OF DOLLARS AND DEFICIT SPENDING

The economywide disruptions caused by the coronavirus are once again bringing forth all the standard macroeconomic panaceas in the form of "activist" monetary and fiscal policies. On Sunday, March 15, the evening before the Monday morning opening of the U.S. stock exchanges, the Federal Reserve announced that it would be buying $500 billion in government treasuries and $200 billion in mortgage-backed securities in the coming weeks and months, basically adding three-quarters of an extra $1 trillion to the American banking system. This is combined with the Federal Reserve's decision to lower its benchmark discount window interest rate (the rate that the Fed charges member banks for short-term lending) to 0.25 percent, in other words, virtually to zero.

At the same time, Congress has passed, and the president has signed, two spending bills as emergency expenditures to counteract negative financial impacts of the coronavirus, additional government expenditures that come to nearly $60 billion—with possibly even a lot more to come. For the first five months of the federal government's current fiscal year (October 2019-February 2020), Uncle Sam has already run a budget deficit of $625 billion, and is projected to run-up a full fiscal year (that will end on September 30, 2020) that will be over $1 trillion before new additions to government spending are accounted for.

The Federal Reserve's "easy money" policy is supposed to stimulate additional private sector investment and related borrowing to boost production and employment. The federal government's additional deficit spending is meant to increase demand to create consumer-end and other sales to increase profit margins as a means to sustain or increase output and jobs.

SUCCESSFUL PRODUCTION COMES BEFORE COORDINATED CONSUMPTION

All of these are stereotypical "Keynesian" policies designed to get an economy out of a recession caused by a falling off of "aggregate demand." But, if anything, the global economy effects from the coronavirus is demonstrating the logic and reality of Say's Law, named after the 19th century French economist, Jean-Baptiste Say (1767-1832). At the end of the day, there is no consumption without production, and, therefore, there is nothing to demand and demand with, without supply.

If you want to eat, you must first plant the crop and wait for it to mature for harvesting at some point in the future. If you want a woolen sweater, you must first raise sheep, wait for their wool to grow, and then after shearing the sheep, manufacture it with all the related inputs into the sweater you'd like to wear. If you want to have something to write with... well, maybe it would be better to just read Leonard Read's famous account in his essay, "I, Pencil." (See my article, "Jean Baptiste Say and the 'Law of Markets.'")[124]

If production falls off, then the ability to either consume directly what you have produced or to sell it to others as your demand for what they may have for sale declines as well. In China first, and now in an increasing number of countries in Europe, people have been told or commanded by their governments to stay home to self-distance themselves from others as a means of minimizing spread of the virus.

To the extent that factories slow or shut down due to work forces remaining home to slow the spread of the virus, the individual outputs of those businesses will decrease or stop; and, therefore, in the aggregate, supply of output as a whole declines, which is only a statistical adding up of all the individual outputs produced by individual firms and enterprises.

Governments cannot be telling people to both curtail their workplace

---

124 Read, Leonard E. "I, Pencil." *Foundation for Economic Education*; Ebeling, Richard M. 2017. "Economic Ideas: Jean-Baptiste Say and the 'Law of Markets.'" *The Future of Freedom Foundation*, June 19.

presence and activities to fight the spread of the virus and, at the same time, maintain their income-based expenditures on the outputs of their national economies. The panic buying that has been seen in many parts of the United States is clearing out existing inventories of goods currently available in retail stores. Replenishing them each day and every week is dependent upon continuing and redirected production reflecting the greater-than-usual relative patterns of consumer demand for what are widely defined as "essentials" and "necessities" in the present crisis atmosphere.

Increasing dollar or nominal spending via greater government deficit spending does nothing to "stimulate" the maintenance of production and employment if workers are quarantined, factories are partly or totally idle, and goods cannot, therefore, be forthcoming in their usual or changed patterns of demand reflecting upon on what the government spends those billions of extra dollars.

Likewise, the presumed attractiveness of zero rates of interest cannot generate real additional investment spending when the available supplies of labor and other factors of production are on the sidelines due to "social distancing" that restricts people's participation in the market. (See my article, "The Myth of Aggregate Demand and Supply".)[125]

FINANCIAL MARKETS WITHOUT AN INTEREST RATE STEERING MECHANISM
We should also not lose sight of the fact that financial markets, due to Federal Reserve policy in recent years and now reinforced with this latest interest rate and security-buying announcement, are operating without a fully functioning price system. Interest rates are meant to be

---

125 Ebeling, Richard M. 2019. "The Myth of Aggregate Demand and Supply." *American Institute for Economic Research*, February 27.

the intertemporal prices to borrow and invest scarce resources across time from willing lenders forgoing the use of their own savings for a period of time.

Zero or near-zero rates of interest must mean either that no one wants to borrow for anything and therefore investment demand is zero, or the economy is so awash in savings that there is more real savings in the economy than a fully satiated investment demand to use that savings for future-oriented production, and therefore savings trades at a zero price. Neither of these conditions can be presumed to hold; that is, either no investment demand of any type for available real savings or so much savings that no investment demand no matter how unprofitable need go unsatisfied from lack of savings.

Of course, we do not fully know what market interest rates should be in either "normal" circumstances or in a virus-based crisis situation like at the present because monetary and credit expansion and interest rate setting and manipulating by the Federal Reserve has and does prevent us from knowing what is the real savings that there may be in the economy and what are the actual market-based profitable investment demands for borrowing at rates of interest formed and set by the interacting forces of supply and demand freed from central bank intervention.

IN SOME UNCHARTED WATERS DUE TO THE CORONAVIRUS CRISIS

In the current climate of public hysteria, mass media hype, and wide-open fiscal and monetary sluice gates, with the possibility of government anti-gouging price controls and "essential goods" rationing, trying to say what policy "X" must and will bring about is impossible to say with complete confidence. But in a situation of declining production due to quarantining and massive increases in potential purchasing power coming on the market via monetary expansion and deficit spending this would suggest, in "normal" times, highly inflationary problems ahead.

But if political pressures bring about municipal, state-level and/or federal systems of price controls and rationing, the result would then be what German economist Wilhelm Röpke (1899-1966) called "repressed inflation." You'd have resource and commodity bottlenecks with shortages of a growing number of those "essential" and non-essential goods, at controlled and fixed prices, with government-directed allocations for goods for production and consumption. The end product would be a system of government central planning, regardless of what the president and Congress decided to call it.

This is, of course, a "worst case" scenario. Chances are it would be a hodge-podge of politically driven incoherent and inconsistent policies introduced on the fly to meet the expediencies and emotions of the moment, and especially in a presidential election year when everyone is desperately pandering for campaign contributions and votes on election day in November.

Or, maybe, the Coronavirus crisis in America will not be as bad and as damaging as many in the scientific community honestly fear. The whole business may blow over in a few months, like other harmful and killer flu seasons. If this, hopefully, turns out to be the case, the whole episode will merely be another teaching moment in misguided and damaging government policies that markets, once again, successfully endured and survived.

THE PARASITES EXACERBATING COVID-19
BY ROBERT E. WRIGHT

March 16, 2020

No, AIER is not breaking science news. The parasites its scholars have in mind infest the body politic, looking to extract resources from others for little or nothing in return. This organization has long complained about these rent-seekers and rent-extractors for decades and it is not about to stop now.

We are not fair-weather libertarians but classical liberals dedicated to truth, justice, and an American Way that seems increasingly under threat. But from the COVID-19 crisis could emerge a new America and a better world if it helps people to perceive reality more clearly. The prospect of death and depression does tend to focus the mind.

Forget about socialism and capitalism. Those terms are simply oversimplifications concocted by academics and activists too lazy or dull to think deeply about economic policies.

Forget, too, about Republican and Democrat politicians. Most stand for nothing but themselves, seeking power for its own sake, or to enrich themselves or their friends and families. Their party platforms are bundles of logical contradictions aimed at electoral victories rather than reforms.

The key to human flourishing is maximizing competition on price and quality on the one hand and on the other minimizing competition for political favor, a.k.a. Parasitism.

To paraphrase a great American statesman, evidence of this dual mandate is written, as with a sunbeam, in the whole volume of human history. To see, just open your mind, let the partisan rage ebb out of your heart, and don't quibble. The claim is not that markets are always perfect and governments always flawed but rather that competition tends to encourage flourishing while parasitism tends to encourage disease.

Only in the last few hundred years have humans flourished *en masse* and only in those places where they managed to kill, evict, chasten, or scotch the biggest parasites of all, the sundry monarchs and dictators who had lorded over most of humanity from the beginning of history. The sundry economic revolutions you may have heard of (agricultural, business, financial, industrial, management, market, technological, transportation, urbanization) were merely the salutary effects of shedding mega-parasites and the consequent redirection of much economic activity away from rent -gathering, -seeking, and -avoidance toward competition on price and quality.

Today, denizens of the world's wealthiest nations all enjoy the benefits of the reformers, revolutionaries, and thinkers who rid their countries of those most obvious and tyrannical parasites. Many lesser worms, however, emerged in the entrails of every body politic, where they have waxed ever larger and more pernicious.

When one country confronts another infected by similar parasites, the tolls the parasites exact largely cancel out and hence remain barely noticeable. One bungling military eventually defeats another (perhaps after years of botched campaigns and millions of deaths) or the lethargic industry of one country gives way to the slightly more vigorous industry of another.

But when humans confront the natural world, the effects of economic parasitism become obvious. Natural disasters decimate nations, like Haiti, still ruled by mega-parasites. Wealthier nations fare better but the weaknesses their lesser worms create or exacerbate remain palpable.

Hurricane Katrina, for example, almost completely destroyed one of North America's gems, New Orleans, because of an ill-fated attempt to centrally plan the Mississippi River and Delta development.

What exactly are these lesser worms and how have they helped to spread COVID-19?

Foremost is a government that has strayed from its original, limited mission of providing pure public goods, services that people want that private producers cannot profitably provide. What goods that entails is not always clear but controlling pandemics is a much better candidate than most other services American governments currently try to provide.

Instead of identifying and focusing on its core mission, the government, like any good parasite, has bloated and stretched itself into so many areas that it is over-extended. Instead of doing a few key things well, it does many, many things it shouldn't be doing at all, and usually poorly at that.

If the U.S. government did not waste so much money on, for example, higher education financing, it could fund the CDC sufficiently to ensure the development of technologies that would automate and speed up viral analysis and vaccination. It should be able to discern in days, not weeks or months, if the best reaction to a new threat is quarantine, herd immunity, or simply information dissemination.[126] This is no pipe dream. It took the Human Genome Project years to sequence the DNA of Homo sapiens but it can now be done in about an hour (which is about where we got with

126 Hanage, William. 2020. "I'm an epidemiologist. When I heard about Britain's 'herd immunity' coronavirus plan, I thought it was satire." *The Guardian*, March 15.

old-fashioned pictures before digital cameras came along).[127]

The fact that medical researchers still do not understand basic tradeoffs between variables like host mortality and viral transmission rate is astounding.[128] Basic science, an area claimed by government, is clearly some combination of insufficiently funded and inefficient, the former due to mission creep and the latter due to the incentive problems endemic in most government endeavors.[129]

The healthcare system is another parasite. Like the government, it gorges itself on an increasing percentage of GDP every year but does not offer an equivalent in return.[130] Both healthcare and higher education work with government to ensure maintenance of the *status quo*, especially restrictions on open competition in terms of price and quality.

Most COVID-19 deaths in the United States to date have occurred in a single facility, one of our nation's numerous poorly run nursing homes.[131] Such facilities abound because of CONS, or certificates of need, government limitations on the number of nursing home beds.[132] If

---

127 Fikes, Bradley J. 2017. "Focus: New machines can sequence human genome in one hour, Illumina announces." *The San Diego Union-Tribune*, January 9.

128 Bull, James J. & Adam S. Lauring. 2014. "Theory and Empiricism in Virulence Evolution." PLoS Pathogens, 10(10): e1004387.

129 Schuck, Peter H. 2015. *Why Government Fails So Often: And How It Can Do Better.* Princeton University Press.

130 Wright, Robert E. 2019. "We Don't Have a Real Market for Health Care in the U.S." *American Institute for Economic Research*, September 19.

131 MacDonald, Heather. 2020. "Compared to what?" *The New Criterion*, March 13.

132 NCSL. 2019. "CON-Certificate of Need State Laws." *National Conference of State Legislators*, January 12.

you don't like the way the nursing home is treating granny, or feel that $8,365 a month for room, board, and a little medical attention is too much, too bad![133] In many states, nobody can lawfully step in to provide a superior service or lower price despite clear empirical evidence that CONs suck the life out of the elderly and cash from their families.[134]

Other problems are more difficult to diagnose. For example, I cannot find antiviral gloves for sale anywhere. They do exist, though they seem to have found only niche acceptance by HCPs and little general public recognition.[135] For some reason unknown to me, nobody had sufficient incentive to develop an affordable commercial product that would actively kill a virus when people voluntarily wearing such gloves automatically clean frequently touched surfaces simply by going about their business.

Regular medical gloves help to protect the wearer and can slow the spread of a virus if worn by a carrier. They can transfer nasties from one surface to another, however, which is why HCPs discard them after each use. A glove treated with an antiviral agent (or anti-bacterial as the case may be), by contrast, would not only prevent transfer, it would micro-clean elevator and other buttons, bathroom doors, and other frequently touched surfaces. And if some genius could get the

---

133 Hoyt, Jeff. 2019. "Nursing Home Costs." *Senior Living*, June 22.

134 Stempniak, Marty. 2018. "Federal report recommends killing certificates of need for nursing homes." *McKnights Longterm Care News*, December 5.

135 Comer, Jason, Trevor Brasel, Bersabeh Tigabu et al. 2015. "Antiviral Activity of Gendine Gloves Against Ebola Virus for Reducing Transmission in Ebola Treatment Settings." *Open Forum Infectious Diseases*, 2(1); Bricout, Fernand, Anne Moraillon, Philippe Sonntag et al. 2003. "Virus-inhibiting surgical glove to reduce the risk of infection by enveloped viruses." *Journal of Medical Virology*, 69(4): 538-545; Reddit. 2020. "Antiviral Gloves." *Reddit*, February.

gloves to work on increasingly ubiquitous touchpads, another source of disease transfer would bite the dust.

Instead, many Americans think effective the human cleaners charged with disinfecting subways and other public places, as if their work could not be undone by one cough, sneeze, or infected bare finger. Our public K-12 education system inculcates in Americans the notion that some benevolent government official can wave a magic wand and protect us all. University study used to disabuse Americans of such notions but, alas, not so much anymore as the academy has fallen into the hands of Left-leaning scholars and administrators.[136]

The so-far easy acceptance of the government's medieval reaction to the spread of a not very lethal virus to a vanishingly small percentage of the population suggests that universities are not helping Americans to overcome the many behavioral biases they inherited from their caveman ancestors.[137]

To be fair, though, buying unusually large amounts of toilet paper may have more to do with Americans' fear of government's response to the virus rather than fear of the virus itself. FDR may have been right that we had nothing to fear but fear itself but his New Deal helped to feed several of the parasites currently weakening Americans' ability to combat COVID-19.

---

136 Brennan, Jason & Phillip Magness. 2019. *Cracks in the Ivory Tower: The Moral Mess of Higher Education*. Oxford University Press.

137 See article herein entitled "Should Government Go Medieval During Pandemic Disease?"; Samson, Alain. 2014. "An Introduction to Behavioral Economics." In *The Behavioral Economics Guide 2014*.

THE ANATOMY OF THE CRASH OF 2020
BY PETER C. EARLE

March 17, 2020.

After decades of predictions, warnings, wagers, prophecies, and what must be many trillions of dollars expended upon short sales, long puts and written calls, hedges and directional bets of every sort: the long-awaited "big Kahuna"—a crash in equities markets—came yesterday.

The Dow Jones Industrial Average closed down 2,997 points to 20,188: a -12.93% one-day decline.

I remember the Crash of '87 (-22.6% in one day), although I wouldn't reach the trading desks in the canyons of Wall Street until a bit less than a decade later. My family didn't have any investments and I really didn't know what to make of it—other than some people in my blue collar, suburban neighborhood seeming to experience a sudden bout of profound, hideous schadenfreude at the "capitalist pigs." I read a bit about it, but resources and life being what they were then, my interest soon faded.

Others, mostly in the media, worried that a recession would shortly follow. One did, but by the time it arrived the Dow Jones Industrial Average was far away from those lows. I was far away, too: Hundreds (and sometimes thousands) of miles from New York City and New Jersey, and about as far from financial markets, derivatives, and trading as one can get: as an infantryman in the United States Army. Markets, the crash, all of it—never part of my life, anyway—couldn't have been further from my mind.

Some years later I returned: not just to the tri-state area, but to the very arenas which not many years before I had heard so much ire and loathing directed at. The Dow was at 5,000, a handful of new "dot com" stocks were undertaking initial public offerings and vaulting to supreme heights on their first day of trading. ("Don't get used to this; it's not usually like this," was the advice frequently offered by older traders.)

Far from being uncommon, volatility came frequently, whether in certain sectors or hitting the entire market. There were concerns about the market rising too quickly, or too slowly; there were debates over valuation, then debates over the debates over valuations; and then a few years in a private hedge fund in Connecticut with a Nobel Prize winner or two as advisors got in big trouble and I saw real market turmoil: rarely the worse for wear, but over time wiser, gaining experience.

There must have been some point at which I asked, or was told, or read, what a "crash" was. Today, any time the market declines sharply, a few hundred points, it's breathlessly described as a crash. What I was told—now decades ago—is that a crash is a decline of more than 10% in a single trading session. Most of what have been called "crashes" have not been. Not the decline when markets re-opened after 9/11 (-7.13%); not the sudden drop when the bailout bill was rejected on September 29th, 2008 (-6.98%); not the May 6, 2010 "Flash Crash" (which doesn't even register in the top 20 of point losses or percentage losses); and certainly nothing that was predicted the day that Trump unexpectedly defeated Hillary Clinton in the 2016 Presidential election. (The day after the election, US equities rose slightly more than 1%.)

Yesterday's fall constitutes a stock market crash. The Crash of '29, which took place over two days—October 28th and 29th, 1929—respectively netted daily returns of -12.82% and -11.73%. Yesterday's fall in prices (as conveyed through stock indices) of -12.93% is bested only by the Crash of 1987 (-22.6%).

A lot of people (people that I know, at least) are saying that a fall of this magnitude is long overdue. Some believe that a sharp, painful decline in indices serves to wring out excesses by driving the "weak hands"—investors or traders with few funds, who are usually leveraged and easily driven to sell—out of the market. Others convey that a price correction of significant magnitude is essential to the continued appreciation of prices. By what measure? There were 58 years between 1929 and 1987, and as someone who saw three-quarters of the period between the 1987 crash and yesterday's: we may not have had a severe decline meeting this particular definition, but we certainly had more than our share of volatility.

Most market declines, and certainly all crashes, bring about some form of political opportunism. For countless Americans to whom tales of the Great Depression were passed, the connection between the Crash of '29 and the ensuing economic collapse is inseparable. (Less successful were attempts to connect the 1987 crash to the 1990-1991 recession.)

CAUSATION

The collapse in '87 has been attributed to many causes, foremost among them automated strategies that had by some accounts become disproportionately impactful forces within financial markets. Often cited among those are portfolio insurance and index arbitrage. And over the years I've met and worked closely with NYSE floor traders who extended the thread of causation to everything from comments made by then-Treasury Secretary James Baker on the weekend before the crash to a number of apocryphal "fat finger" errors.

Exactly this again. Algorithms, derivatives, "speculators," "greed," margin calls, the lack of a fabled "Plunge Protection Team" to act, villainous hedge funds, and every other pathetic explanation or conspiracy theory will, over the next few months, be dragged out, dusted off, and touted to explain the recent declines.

The better explanation is vastly simpler.

Since Trump's election, there has been a contingent who have sought to blame the President any time the market declines; many of them simultaneously, and shamelessly, crediting Obama for the longer-term bull market and the strong economy. Having said that, a decisive portion of yesterday's historic decline—the second largest percentage decline ever for the Dow Jones Industrial Average, and the largest ever for the NASDAQ—should be laid at the feet of Trump. The original plan, evidently, was to hold the press conference—a release of updates from the Coronavirus Task Force—at 10:30am; the meeting was then moved to 3:30pm before being moved back to 3:15pm. In any case, the current administration seems to have not learned from countless previous Administrations that news which is likely to foment volatility is better delivered after market hours. Oval Office addresses (and other major announcements) have typically been made at 8pm EST to maximize viewership, not interrupt dinners or after-school activities, and not unnecessarily roil markets.

Whether the President's advisors are unaware of that or he for whatever reason refused to heed them, it comes across, flatly, as bumbling and amateur. A look at the intraday chart from yesterday tells the tale: the market was down on the day, and mostly stable—down between 7 and 8 percent for most of the afternoon. And with a few comments about a recession in the immediate future, and additional comments about essentially shutting down the U.S. economy until August, we find ourselves here: with the first stock market crash of the 21st century, 33 years after the last one.

REMEMBER WHAT'S REAL

It is not exactly true, as is often said at these times, that stock prices and volatility in various financial markets have no bearing upon, or don't reflect, the "real world." Most people, understandably, don't make the connection between things they encounter in their daily lives and such arcane economic functions as price discovery, fund mobilization, capital formation, and the provision of liquidity, but they would certainly feel their absence.

Certainly, people close to retirement who are depending on their 401Ks and IRAs will rightfully be concerned about their financial wherewithal after the drawdown of the last few days—in particular, yesterday. And no doubt across the vast diaspora of financial market participants, professional and amateur, yesterday's drop made and broke fortunes.

The crash, though—in fact, all of the recent tumult in equity, fixed income, derivative, commodity, and crypto markets—is just the scenery, as it was in 1987 and 1929. If a recession is on its way, it was with or without yesterday's sharp downturn. The more critical elements are the fear mongering all around us and the seeming effort of politicians from mayors to governors to heads of state to one-up each other in draconian measures.

Domestic military deployments—whatever their rationalization—should chill the spine more than a stock cut down by 25% in a matter of days. And no, most unfortunately, it is not surprising that once again the American people are being told that a massive spending bill must be passed to save the world—without a word of discussion, and absent transparency. In different words, just over ten years after the last time, the colossally insulting banality that a bill "has to be passed to see what's in it" is again quickly taking form.

The real history of this crash is that the market began to fall exactly as the political class began to panic, speak of shutdowns, demand flight cancellations, talk of closing up and stopping history. Whatever you think about the virus threat, and even if you think all this is justified in the name of stopping the spread, let's not be confused about what drove this disaster from the beginning: the fear that politics would attack commercial society at its root.

For some years ago, the apocalyptic mentality has been gaining in our politics, with the right wing screaming about rampant immorality, globalism, and the breakdown of nations, while the left has been calling for the end of fossil fuels, wealth, and capitalism itself. They share a common enemy, the free and peaceful commercial society that empowers individuals over collectives. That the social order that has made everyone rich must be destroyed is something on which they agree. And now these gangs are demanding your allegiance in a time of grave crisis.

The calamity before our eyes is beginning to look like some version of their imagined dystopia while the rest of us are left to struggle through this disaster the old-fashioned way, not with ideological delusion but with intelligence, calm, and rational planning for the future. There is indeed a virus among us, one far more damaging than that which goes by the name COVID-19.

A POLITICALLY FUELED PANIC IS NOT A GOOD PLAN
BY MICHA GARTZ

March 17, 2020

My mum has been sending me daily messages from Australia, asking if I had stocked up yet. She's sent me lists of items to keep on hand, and videos of hysterical shoppers getting close to all-out brawls in supermarket aisles over toilet paper.

She has seen supermarkets get steadily emptier, and runs leaving shelves normally full of basic items such as rice and paper-towel bare for two weeks now. I had largely disregarded her advice—there's no way supply chains will be interrupted, and the US has been calm so far.

This was, until Sunday, when I heard that there are police stationed at fuel stations in DC as a measure "to keep the peace." Going to the store, I began to notice how busy it was. People were cutting one another off to get to aisels (hopefully) full of rice, pasta, and yes, toilet paper.

YOU'RE DAMNED IF YOU DO, AND YOU'RE DAMNED IF YOU DON'T.

While I don't believe supply chains will be interrupted, hearing prominent politicians and journalists thunder over the radio that, if you're not doing something to prepare, you're doing something wrong. This, obviously won't help anyone. If people panic and begin stockpiling then those that don't stockpile may very well leave the store empty handed.

While I pity the poor person, who, on their last role goes for their weekly shop to find that toilet paper has completely vanished, I also find the mental image of hoarders with piles of mint-in-pack TP piled up to the ceiling absolutely hilarious. So, much to my mother's relief, I bought a few extra days' worth of food amidst a grocery store backdrop of stirring panic.

We seem to assume that the human race is so evolved, that we're so civilized now compared to our cave-dwelling forebearers. Until there's something like a natural disaster or pandemic to start frenzied hoarding and panic.

I wonder what will happen to food pantries: are (or will) we, in our panic, decide to start taking from public food pantries? Certainly people will donate less to these facilities, which are intended to serve those who are homeless, impoverished, or facing food insecurity. If we see canned goods disappear from shelves, will we compromise our values and start raiding their canned goods and non-perishables?

These preparations, so out of the ordinary, are more reminiscent of war-times than the modern prosperity we've come to enjoy.

My grandmother from Germany remembers the war, and grew up poor. She laughed at our concern about going on holiday with a few other octogenarians for ten days. *Of course she'll still go*! Contrast that with my mother who, having been through constant shortages on various goods (including toilet paper) during her childhood in Zimbabwe, is now hiding tinned tomatoes around the house.

My grandmother is not the only fearless person about. A corona-patient in Kentucky has steadfastly refused to self-isolate, under 24-hour guard.[138] This is not the first instance of someone refusing what is essentially house-arrest: a few days ago a father from Missouri reportedly disregarded a home quarantine request in order to attend

138 Desrochers, Daniel. 2020. "One of two new Kentucky coronavirus cases refused to self-isolate. He's being forced." *Lexington Herald Leader*, March 14.

a father-daughter dance at a nearby hotel.[139] The consequent public outlash on social media, and reports of a police patrol to protect the family in their home following the incident seem to indicate that we are not particularly civilized.

THE 'DO SOMETHING-OR-DIE' APPROACH

It would be political suicide to do nothing, even when in instances when that is the best option. Invoking a 'state of emergency' to give legal impetus to quarantine 'free spirits' may help prevent an immediate destruction of your political career, but it makes things worse in the long-run.

Now also seems to be a good excuse for socialist tendencies to crawl out of the woodwork. Billions in emergency funds are being released, there will probably be millions in lawsuits, and politicians are using the emotional heat around Covid-19 to promote ideologically-based initiatives such as mass bail-outs and nationalization of companies.

Some elected representatives, such as New York City Mayor Bill de Blasio, are calling for the nationalization of 'critical private companies' in order to keep them running 24/7.[140] Anyone who's had to deal with any government service, from DVS and the Social Security Administration to getting operating approval for their businesses will probably shudder at the thought. Excluding services such as law enforcement, I struggle to think of a government department that operates outside of the hours of 9-5 Monday-Friday.

---

139 Iati, Marisa. 2020. "County says a father ignored a coronavirus quarantine directive. His lawyer says he was never told." *The Washington Post*, March 10.

140 Blitzer, Ronn. 2020. "De Blasio urges 'nationalization' of key industries, calls coronavirus outbreak a 'war-like situation'." *Fox News*, March 16.

ALTERNATIVE PROPOSITION:

While shutting things down seems logical—at least superficially—forcibly closing restaurants, schools and borders would force the very thing the government does not want: large crowds of people in a confined area—such as supermarkets or airports.

Arguably, the best thing we could do (for those who are healthy and unconcerned) both for our health and the sake of the economy, would be to continue our lives as normal. If we eat at (or get takeaway from) restaurants and cafes, continue to let children play with friends, and cut back on visiting elderly parents, we—and our economy—will come out stronger for it.

I'm curious to see the government try implement price controls on grocery items, although realistically this a) wouldn't work and would eventually lead to rationing if supply chains really are interrupted, and b) we might hear de Blasio call for nationalization of grocery stores. At that point I think we can truly say we've lost our 'free' institutions.

STUCK IN THE MIDDLE

If travel restrictions and home-quarantine is being enacted out of compassion for our neighbours, then there also exist compassionate reasons against such restrictive measures.

There are plenty of poor travellers, stranded either indefinitely in a foreign country half-way home, or seeking a third country to reside in for two week 'quarantine' periods in the hopes that this country won't also be added to the ban.

Those about to move abroad to start work may wonder how long their job will be waiting for them. Even more tragically, those with vulnerable family members face a significant problem: what if their loved-one becomes seriously ill (with corona or something else) and you can't make it to them for their last few days of life?

CORONA: UNDERMINING EFFECTIVE FUTURE RESPONSES TO PANDEMICS

So far, the numbers of deaths/infections are not as terrible as first predicted: the virus isn't causing perfectly healthy people to drop dead, serious cases remain relatively low and the virus is primarily affecting those who are frail or have underlying health conditions. The resultant frustration felt by those who lose their incomes, who are forced to cancel conferences and events, shutter their businesses or stay home from school may undermine future efforts to address pandemics.[141]

If we believe we are civilized, we must question why we need to 'go medieval.'[142] Is it simply to alleviate public fears? Supermarket shelves seem to indicate that it is having the opposite effect. Indeed, it could have disastrous consequences down the road: an over-reaction to contagious diseases which are later perceived as not-so-serious will undermine future efforts at containment.

One day we may have an outbreak of highly contagious disease X which kills every person it comes into contact with on the 60th day of being infected. If that happens we may initially approach the situation more hesitantly than we should by refusing to shut things down or quarantine because, "don't you remember the over-reaction to Covid-19?"

141 Tucker, Jeffrey A. 2020. "Why this Draconian Response to COVID-19?" *American Institute for Economic Research*, March 8; Ellyatt, Holly. 2020. "Italy closes bars, restaurants and most shops as coronavirus death toll jumps 30%." *CNBC News*, March 12.

142 See article herein entitled "Should Government Go Medieval During Pandemic Disease?" *American Institute for Economic Research*, March 4; See article herein entitled "The Parasites Exacerbating COVID-19."

Critically, information remains opaque, hysteria is growing exponentially, but deaths are not (at least for present). Ultimately, if the data doesn't match the rhetoric, government actions may be a present embodiment of the story of the boy who cried wolf.

LIVING WITH CRISIS

AN EPISTEMIC CRISIS

BY JEFFREY TUCKER

March 17, 2020.

This pandemic crisis is not only about health and economics; we are also experiencing an epistemic meltdown. The core question concerns: knowledge. Information. Accurate information. What are the risks? The infection and death rates? The demographics? The geography of the spread? How contagious, how deadly, how can we know, and how can we find out? Who can we trust with such wildly divergent opinions out there?

Everyone is doing their best poring over the data we have and can access thanks to digital media, places such as OurWorldinData, simply because the government's official page at the CDC doesn't provide enough data and its employees apparently take off for the weekend.[143] Based on what we see, the infection rates are falling, defying the direst predictions. But the data are incomplete: testing is not universal, incubation rates are uncertain (5 to 14 days), and data in general rely on collection, which is itself an unscientific enterprise.

But think about the following. Above all else, the number one question people have in this crisis is: do I have the Coronavirus? This more than anything else is the central concern. Remarkably, Americans did not know and had no means of finding out. The reason is now clear: the Centers for Disease Control had previously nationalized all disease testing. A government bureaucracy like any other. It's hardly

---

143 Roser, Max, Hannah Ritchie, Esteban Ortiz-Ospina. "Coronavirus Disease (COVID-19) – Statistics and Research." *Our World in Data*, March 19; CDC. 2020. "Cases in U.S." *Centers for Disease Control and Prevention*, March 19.

surprising that it completely flopped.

AIER already explained how a private researcher, funded by the Bill & Melinda Gates Foundation, was forcibly prevented from producing and distributing a valid test.[144] The CDC said no.

Now, more details are rolling in about how all this went down, thanks to intrepid reporters who smelled a rat. The CDC in the first week of February sent 160,000 tests to labs around the country. The tests were faulty and produced confusing results. They were withdrawn, just as private laboratories fixed the test.

Still, no approval was being given for private labs to produce tests. For the very curious, you can read the many stories of private labs who were begging for a chance to do something about the problem.[145] The red tape, confusion, power struggles, and information blockages are being documented by the day.[146]

The Washington Post reports:[147]

> The U.S. efforts to distribute a working test stalled until Feb. 28, when federal officials revised the CDC test and began loosening up FDA rules that had limited who could develop coronavirus diagnostic tests.

---

144 See the article herein entitled "How the US Botched Coronavirus Testing."

145 Baird, Robert P. 2020. "What Went Wrong with Coronavirus Testing in the U.S." *The New Yorker*, March 16.

146 Khazan, Olga. 2020. "The 4 Key Reasons the U.S. Is So Behind on Coronavirus Testing." *The Atlantic*, March 13.

147 Whoriskey, Peter, Neena Satija. 2020. "How U.S. coronavirus testing stalled: Flawed tests, red tape and resistance to using the millions of tests produced by the WHO." *The Washington Post*, March 16.

The CDC/FDA bans on private tests were done in the name of health and safety. That was the period in which panic enveloped the nation. No one knew. We had no means to find out. Everyone and everything flipped out. We replaced knowledge with insanity.

F.A. Hayek was right that the use of knowledge in society is the central issue in economic and social organization. We had been cut off from the knowledge flow that otherwise would have been ours had we left this issue entirely to the private sector, which would have brought a Coronavirus test to you as quickly as you can order a pizza.

Instead, there was nothing but confusion.[148]

> Shortly after Feb. 28, when CDC officials announced the decision to reconfigure the CDC test, the number of those tests run by public health labs soared, from roughly 25 or fewer per day to as many as 1,500. At the same time, authorities were allowing other facilities to use their own tests—including Cleveland Clinic, Stanford and Greninger's at the University of Washington.
>
> Even so, complaints of testing scarcity continued to roll in last week. As tests become more widely available, experts and officials have cautioned that a backlog will continue because of critical shortages: swabs to collect patient samples, machines to extract the genetic material from the swabs, workers qualified to run the tests.
>
> Even if those problems are resolved, however, those critical early delays, when the CDC was struggling to issue tests to the states, significantly damaged efforts to contain the spread of the

---

148 *Ibid.*

coronavirus, experts said.

In a CDC tele-briefing on Feb. 29 that included some local and state public health directors, local officials lamented the initial inability to test. A reporter asked: "Did the lack of testing capabilities delay finding out who these cases were, particularly the person who died?"

In answering, Jeff Duchin, the public health chief in King County, Wash., where 37 deaths have been reported, suggested the lack of tests was critical, in addition to the fact that authorities had limited who could be tested. Initially, they had said tests would only be used for those who had traveled in affected regions of the globe or had otherwise been in contact with an infected person.

Another report adds:[149]

The void created by the CDC's faulty tests made it impossible for public-health authorities to get an accurate picture of how far and how fast the disease was spreading. In hotspots like Seattle, and probably elsewhere, COVID-19 spread undetected for several weeks, which in turn only multiplied the need for more tests.

Lacking that knowledge, public officials freaked out. Stay home. Keep your distance. Everyone is a suspect. Anyone and everyone could be positive for Corona. Socially shame anyone out and about.

---

149 Baird (2020).

Board up the bars![150]

It was this sense, along with utter panic on the part of public officials, that led the markets to crash. After all, you can't have an economy if people cannot engage and trade, can't go to work, can't distribute goods and services, and forget about investment.

And here we find the key to understanding why this Coronavirus has produced a social and economic calamity, whereas the H1N1 (Swine flu) from ten years ago is barely remembered by most people. It came and went with a large health cost (infections: 57 million; fatalities 12,469) but low cost otherwise. The critical difference was that the CDC worked with private laboratories and medical facilities to get the test out there. A few public schools closed for part of the day but there was no panic, no large economic loss.[151]

In the midst of all of this, this panic learning and trying, this speculation and searching, this mass national confusion, this endless and chaotic longing to know, this constant grasping for intelligence, one thing became certain: states at all levels decided to act. As if they knew the right course. And they acted with extreme force. And their message was always the same: stop whatever you are doing and do nothing instead.

This was and is the ultimate expression of nihilism, the chaos that follows ignorance. Officials in this country decided to shut down society—as if this were even possible—as a replacement for reliable,

---

150 Woods, Amanda. 2020. "Cincinnati police board up bar that defied coronavirus shutdown order." *New York Post*, March 17.

151 Ioannidis, John P. A. 2020. "A fiasco in the making? As the coronavirus pandemic takes hold, we are making decisions without reliable data." *Stat*, March 17.

usable, actionable knowledge that we were all forcibly prevented from gaining when we most needed it.

It's a classic pretension of knowledge about which the government itself is clueless. They tried to plan without reliable signs or signals. That's a recipe for chaotic, hasty, haphazard, and internally contradictory policy decisions, all driven by the need to maintain the appearance of an official response.

Such circumstances are rips for abuse. Contrary perspectives, such as that offered by Stanford bio-statistician John P.A. Ionnidis, were ignored.[152] In his view, we have absolutely no basis to assume that any existing models are right, and that the fatality rate could be extremely low (0.025%). Were these views ignored because he doesn't have the right conclusion?

We got censorship of the problem when it first emerged, and now other governments trying to cover their own rears for chaotic inaction as it's played out. Then all the vultures arrive, trying to append their pet political projects to the response: authoritarian busybodies like Cuomo and de Blasio instinctually calling out the police or calling for nationalization of industry, Bernie using it to make the case for Medicare for All, the UBI crowd trying to build that into a stimulus, the nationalists demanding a shutdown of global trade.

Right now, there is a huge debate in this country about how bad Coronavirus really is. Some people are saying that we are all going to be infected. Many will die. Others are saying that this is completely overwrought, that authorities have overreacted, and that viruses burn themselves out and that the casualties will be few. The problem here is

---

152 *Ibid.*

that we haven't had access to reliable, scientifically valid information either to avoid panic and behave in a rational way.

The contrast with South Korea, where infections have fallen and fallen, is striking.[153] There were no shutdowns, no geographic quarantines, no panics. Society was open for business. Life went on as normal but for one thing: people had access to testing, which is to say that people were given access to the essential and most important piece of information that was necessary at the time.

That was not the case in the US.

And that is a major source of the problem. The information problem turns out to be critical for the survival of economic life, exactly as F.A. Hayek discovered in the 20th century.[154] Those information flows, when they are cut off by force, for whatever reason, and in whatever form, lead to chaos. A tragic and deeply damaging chaos.

The ray of hope is that reliable tests are going to be distributed widely in the coming days, and that will solve the great epistemic crisis created by the CDC/FDA. There is hope and light at the end of this very dark tunnel of ignorance.

Update: sure enough, as testing has improved in the US, reported death rates are falling, and could eventually reach that of Germany, which is the same as the seasonal flu.[155]

---

153 See article herein entitled "South Korea Preserved the Open Society and Now Infection Rates are Falling." *American Institute for Economic Research*, March 12.

154 Hayek, Friedrich A. 1945. "The Use of Knowledge in Society." *American Economic Review*, XXXV(4): 519-530.

155 See article herein entitled "The US Coronavirus Death Rate Is Falling, and Germany's More So."

IF YOU BAIL OUT EVERYONE, YOU BAIL OUT NO ONE
BY JOHN TAMNY

March 18, 2020.

It's sad any of this needs to be said or written, but it cannot be stressed enough that government outlays are a consequence of growth that's *already taken place*. The federal budget in the U.S. is the largest in the world, and the U.S. Treasury can borrow trillions more, precisely because Congress and Treasury are backed by some of the most productive people on earth.

Which brings us to a recent conservative editorial making a case for former Fed Governor Kevin Warsh's call for the Federal Reserve to "create a new facility that could lend to companies hit by the economic shutdown." Warsh walks on water in conservative circles, which may explain why what is so contradictory to economic logic is gaining so much traction on the right.

Indeed, as the same conservative editorial made plain, "state and federal leaders are shutting down the American economy." Goodness, the editorial was titled "Financing an Economic Shutdown."[156]

The shutdown aspect of the lapse of reason we're all suffering from politicians and those in their employ rates constant mention in consideration of conservative calls for a "new facility" to bolster businesses whacked by political ineptitude. Those businesses, and those in the employ of those businesses, would normally fund government outlays but for one problem: politicians are in the process of shutting down

---

156 WSJ. 2020. "Financing an Economic Shutdown." *The Wall Street Journal*, March 16.

the economy for weeks, and perhaps even months.

It's seemingly been glossed over by Warsh and other conservatives that government spending is just another word for private sector spending orchestrated by politicians. All wealth is created in the private sector only for government to politicize spending of this private sector wealth creation to the tune of $4 to $5 trillion per year. The growth once again *already happened*, hence the ability of Nancy Pelosi, Mitch McConnell et al to spend.

Implicit in the grand plan promoted by Warsh and fellow conservatives is that the federal government and the Fed it created have resources all their own, waiting patiently to be mobilized in times of trouble. No. That's not serious. Those Warsh et al would like to save are the ones that, if politicians weren't limiting their ability to work and produce, would provide the funds for Warsh et al to mis-allocate. Production first, then government waste. Warsh and modern conservatives seem to have skipped the class on Say's Law.

Taking this bad dream further, the conservative editorial acknowledges what's true, that government is approaching the Coronavirus "health crisis" with "command-and-control emergency powers." Translated, city, state and federal politicians are shutting down the economy, presumably for our own good. Or at least what they presume to be our own good.

Considering the above with various federal lending programs top of mind, do the conservatives supporting this massive federal intervention remember the track record of past "command and control" economies? That they were thoroughly downtrodden is one of those blinding glimpses of the obvious. This then raises a question of which investors, of the private sector variety, would lend or invest in size fashion into an economy that's in the process of being taken over by hysterical politicians on all levels? The question answers itself, at which point one must ask why taxpayers must be forced to lend toward an economy that a private sector investor wouldn't touch.

To which one assumes conservatives will reply per the editorial that this is a "liquidity panic," and since it is, the federal government must step in. Except that tight liquidity is a market signal like any other; in this case one logically signaling horror on the part of investors that politicians on all levels are in the process of forcing a centrally planned economic reversal on the most dynamic economy in the world. Conservatives claim to revere market signals, market signals are presently telling politicians to stop the economic asphyxiation they're forcing on the economy, but conservatives want taxpayers to blunt the signal?

One would think conservatives would have learned their lesson from 2008 when, amid their clamor for bailouts, markets spoke anyway. Logically they spoke quite a bit more harshly thanks to the interventions. Yet conservatives want the same to take place again? You can't make this up. Capital is already scarce thanks to political ineptitude, so the conservative solution is for government to oversee the waste of even more on loans that no private investor would dare touch?

It's been said regularly in this column before, but needs to be said again: the central planning that fails in flamboyant fashion during good times fails even more impressively during bad times. Yet the ideology most rhetorically associated with free markets and free minds is presently calling for government to plan the resource allocation for the economy that it's in the process of shutting down. You really, *really* can't make this up.

All of which brings us to the justification for this mass handover of power to government. The economic shutdown that the quoted editorial suggests could be measured in months is explained away by those editorialists as "prudent," and as "a health measure to 'flatten the curve' of infections." Oh wow. Let's please unpack this. We're being told that the very humans who have created awe-inspiring prosperity, who've lifted billions out of the most desperate of living conditions, and who've created all manner of cures for diseases that used to kill and maim, are now a *danger* to one another.

Yes, that's what we've come to hear of politicians, economists, alarmist scientists, and their editorialist enablers on the left and right: we the people are a lethal menace to one another, and since we are, we must give our liberty and prosperity away to politicians until such a time that they deem it ok for us to have it back. This *political* tragedy that's wrecking the economy is real, and it's *heartbreaking*.

GOOD REASONS TO DOUBT THE ESTIMATE OF COVID-19 DEATHS
BY WILLIAM J. LUTHER

March 18, 2020.

A recent study from the Imperial College COVID-19 Response Team estimates that as many as 2.2 million Americans could die from the coronavirus (COVID-19).[157] Its estimates come from an epidemiological model which, among other things, takes into account the strain on hospitals that is expected if we are unable to flatten the curve.[158]

The *New York Times* credits the study with changing the tone at the White House, which revised its guidance on gathering limits from 50 to 10 on Sunday and urged Americans to increase social distance.[159]

That headline number—2.2 million deaths in the US—has received a lot of attention. As the authors of the study note, however, that estimate only results in "the (unlikely) absence of any control measures or spontaneous changes in individual behavior." In other words, it is the study's worst-case scenario, where everyone just goes on as if there were no virus even though people around them are getting sick and dying.

Perhaps the authors should have written "incredibly unlikely" and not put it in parentheticals. Again, the estimate is based on the

---

157 Ferguson, Niel M., Daniel Laydon, Gemma Nedjati-Gilani et al. 2020. "Impact of non-pharmaceutical interventions (NPIs) to reduce COVID19 mortality and healthcare demand." *Imperial College COVID-19 Response Team*, March 16.

158 Specktor, Brandon. 2020. "Coronavirus: What is 'flattening the curve,' and will it work?" *LiveScience*, March 16.

159 Fink, Sheri. 2020. "White House Takes New Line After Dire Report on Death Toll." *The New York Times*, March 16.

implausible assumption that we do nothing. And, by "do nothing," I do not mean "fail to adopt a meaningful government response." There would need to be "no spontaneous changes in individual behavior" (i.e., those not directed by the government) as well.

Such an estimate might provide a useful starting point. In particular, it might give us some perspective on the absolute upper bound of reasonable estimates. But it should not be taken as a reasonable expectation of what will actually happen. Remember the Lucas critique: when circumstances change, people change their behavior.[160] The headline estimate merely recognizes how bad it would be in the absence of any such behavioral or policy changes.

I cannot overemphasize how implausible the headline estimate is. We cannot "do nothing" at this point because we are *already doing more than nothing.* We are isolating those infected, banning travel from high-risk countries, self-quarantining the at-risk, working remotely, closing schools, increasing social distance, washing hands more frequently, … And those control measures and behavioral responses are precisely the kind of steps the study's authors go on to consider.

If anything, I would say the study gives us some reasons to be optimistic. The authors estimate a 15 to 30 percent reduction in deaths from just two, small changes:

- Case isolation in the home
- Social distancing of entire population

---

160 Wikipedia. 2020. "Lucas critique." *Wikipedia*, March 4.

Moreover, the authors are relatively conservative in modeling these changes. For example, they assume isolation reduces contact outside the home by just 75 percent and that only 70 percent of those experiencing symptoms actually respond by isolating.

They assume social distancing reduces contact outside the home, school, or workplace by 75 percent, but that school contact rates are unchanged and workplace contact rates are reduced by just 25 percent.

The authors estimate a 49 to 50 percent reduction in deaths from three changes:

- Case isolation in the home
- Voluntary home quarantine
- Social distancing of those over 70 years of age

Voluntary home quarantine differs from case isolation in that *all* household members stay home following the identification of symptoms, not just the person (or, case) showing symptoms. And, as in the previous scenario, the assumptions concerning compliance are conservative. Only 50 percent of people are assumed to voluntarily quarantine when one of their family members becomes ill.

More strikingly, in this scenario, those of us under age 70 without symptoms or family members with symptoms are assumed to go on about our lives as if there isn't a virus killing a bunch of people. We do not work remotely. We do not cancel upcoming trips. We do not increase social distance. We do not wash our hands more frequently. There is no behavioral response. It is just business as usual for most of us. That strikes me as implausible. And, the more we change our behaviors in response, the fewer deaths will result.

To recap, with three not-so-incredible responses, the authors of the Imperial College study estimate that we will reduce deaths from 2.2 million to 1.1 million. That is still a lot of deaths, to be sure. It is roughly 32 times as many deaths as resulted from the flu last year.

However, we should keep in mind that the estimates produced in the study are based on relatively conservative assumptions about our responses and how the disease will spread in the US. I have written a lot about the former already, so let me now briefly consider the latter.

The authors implicitly assume that COVID-19 will move from person to person in the US just as it did in China and South Korea. However, we have learned that proximity matters a lot with this disease. A recent report from the World Health Organization (WHO) found that most human-to-human transmission of COVID-19 in China occurred in families.[161]

Part of the reason why diseases spread so rapidly in places like China and South Korea is because there are so many people living so closely together. Despite vast rural areas, population density in China is still roughly 375 people per square mile. In Wuhan, where COVID-19 broke out, it is around 3,379 people per square mile. In South Korea, there are some 1,302 people per sq mile. And, in Seoul, its capital, there are 41,655 people per sq mile.

The US is much less densely populated than China and South Korea and Americans are much more likely to live alone. In the US, there are just 90 people per square mile. We have high-density areas, like New York City, where there are roughly 27,751 people per square mile. But most cities in the US are more like Columbus, OH—3,960 people per square mile. And most places in the US are not cities. That means, at least outside of a few large cities, COVID-19 will have fewer direct,

161 WHO. 2020. "Report of the WHO-China Joint Mission on Coronavirus Disease 2019 (COVID-19)." *World Health Organization*, February 16-24.

personal contact points to spread from person to person in the US.

Based on my reading of the Imperial College COVID-19 Response Team study, I conclude that 1.1 million is a plausible high-end estimate of the number of deaths in the event that we take no extreme measures and only partially comply with sensible measures. In addition to the estimate, however, there are three key takeaways.

First, none of the responses considered above requires government action. We can choose to isolate when we experience symptoms. The family members of those who fall ill can choose to quarantine themselves. We can choose to increase social distance. We do not need the government to force us to do those things.

It is also not merely a matter of individual choice, though. There is a big role for civil and commercial society to play. We can advise others to wash their hands more frequently; to make one trip to the grocery store per week rather than three; and to stand further apart when we talk. We can shun and shame those who refuse to heed our advice. We can postpone unnecessary social gatherings, or move them online.[162] We can come up with novel business solutions, like carving our special times for those most at-risk to shop.[163] We can share best practices for working remotely and provide resources to others in our field who are transitioning away from face-to-face encounters.[164]

---

162 NYT. 2020. "Social Lives are Moving Online as the U.S. Adjusts to the Coronavirus." *The New York Times*, March 18.

163 Tyko, Kelly. 2020. "Stores designate shopping time for seniors vulnerable amid coronavirus: Walmart, Target, Whole Foods and more." *USA Today*, March 18.

164 Bernick, Michael. 2020. "Remote Work and Best Practices: The Coronavirus Workplace Series." *Forbes*, March 16; Tabarrok, Alex. 2020. "MRU and the Coronavirus." *Marginal Revolution*, March 13.

Consider some further examples from my personal experience. My employer has required any employee who has recently traveled abroad to self-quarantine for 14 days. Will I be shot or sent to prison if I refuse? No. But, in a state with at-will employment, I could lose my job. At the very least, I would receive some disappointing glances and perhaps justifiably unkind words from colleagues for putting them all at risk. So I am working from home, waiting it out.

My gym, which is usually packed and sweaty for a few classes each day, has capped the number of participants at 12 per class and significantly increased the number of classes offered to accommodate. For folks hunkered down like me, they have rolled out a separate program that can be completed at home with no equipment and little space. No doubt these efforts were difficult to develop quickly and more costly to provide than the usual services. But the owners care about the community they have built. And they are led by the profit motive to provide the services their customers demand.

Can government policies limit the spread of COVID-19 further still? Sure. The government has one core competency: it can use force. And, in most cases, it can force us to do more of something than we would do on our own. But we should be hesitant to permit use of that force. As a liberal, I strongly believe in the presumption of liberty.[165] That does not mean it is never acceptable to coerce others. Rather, it means that it is only acceptable to coerce others when there is a very good reason for doing so.

With a presumption of liberty, each person is mostly free to choose the extent to which they interact with others or engage in isolation.

---

165 Libertarianism. 2008. "Liberty, Presumption of." *Libertarianism.org*, August 15.

However, if one tests positive for or is exhibiting obvious symptoms of COVID-19, then it is justifiable to impose isolation on that individual and those they have closely interacted with for a reasonable period of time, under humane conditions. In cases where it is less clear that coercion is warranted, however, we should err on the side of liberty.

The second key takeaway is that the relevant trade-offs depend crucially on local conditions. Outside of a few high-population-density urban areas, the cost of shutting everything down—in terms of real hardships for real people—is almost certainly unwarranted. We do not want the virus to spread. But we also do not want a cure that is worse than the disease.

Furthermore, the second takeaway suggests we should be looking for more decentralized solutions. The most appropriate policy response will probably vary from place to place. COVID-19 poses less risk to Omaha (3,378 people per square mile) than Chicago (11,841 per square mile). And it poses even less risk to rural areas. In Scioto County, OH, where I grew up, there are just 130 people per square mile. A one-size-fits-all approach will almost certainly result in far more costs than are warranted.

There are certainly things that federal and state governments can do to reduce the spread COVID-19 and mitigate the economic burden for the least well off. They can collect and provide information, especially insofar as it relates to issues that cross jurisdictions. They can trace the close connections of those infected and support isolation efforts when warranted. They can delay when tax payments are due. But much of what needs to be done can—and should—be done locally.

The third key takeaway is that small behavioral changes can really add up. Recall that the study made relatively conservative assumptions about compliance and, yet, resulted in significant reductions in the total number of deaths in the US. It follows that we can probably limit the number of deaths even further than those estimated in the study by increasing compliance with sensible measures. If you can work remotely, you probably should work remotely. Instead of dining at a restaurant, order take-out. And wash your hands every 90 minutes, setting a timer if you are prone to forget. These small changes impose small costs. But they seem to yield outsized benefits.

To many, the Imperial College COVID-19 Response Team study is taken to mean the end of the world is nigh. Having read the report, I offer a very different conclusion. It suggests small, personal sacrifices are warranted; local businesses must come up with innovative solutions; communities should postpone large social gatherings until the storm has passed; and governments ought to trace the close connections of those infected and require isolation when warranted. The study is not the last word on the subject. Indeed, other scientists are already weighing in, discussing its strengths and weaknesses. But it is a sober assessment of the most pressing problem facing the world right now. And we should share and discuss it with the same level of sobriety.

THE DIFFERENCE BETWEEN A RECESSION AND A CRACK-UP
BY JOHN TAMNY

March 19, 2020.

Howard Marks has long made the point that the seeds of bad economic times are planted during the good times, and the seeds of good during bad. Marks's correct vision of recession and recovery needs to be discussed in the here and now.

Considering good or booming economic times, it's not unreasonable to suggest that the individuals who comprise any economy sometimes develop bad personal and work habits. At the same time, companies reach in terms of how they expand, the individuals they hire, along with how many they hire.

Banks and investment banks similarly are forced to reach somewhat. Precisely because there's more competition to make loans, and to finance new and existing companies, capital allocators reach too. So do they with investments. That they do is somewhat logical. Money flows and lending may be denominated in dollars, but they signal the movement of goods, services and labor. During good times production of goods and services grows, as frequently do labor forces, and all of this is revealed through credit expansion.

Recessions, far from a terrifying sign, actually just signal a broad realization of errors by individuals and corporations. Recessions signal recovery precisely because they signal the correction of the mistakes made during the good times.

That they do explains the corollary to Marks's point: during troubled times we lay the groundwork for better. Yet again errors are corrected of the expansion, hiring, investment and lending variety, bad personal habits are nipped, bad hires that don't fit for companies and individuals alike are released into the market economy in search of better matches, plus individuals and businesses shore up their personal financial situations.

Some Keynesian thinkers in the economics profession believe consumption powers economic growth, but as the mildly sentient among us know well, investment is the true driver of growth. Crucial about investment is that it's a logical consequence of savings, which explains why good times emerge from the bad. As individuals and corporations shrink their outgoings, capital formation grows, thus setting the stage for growing amounts of investment that puts an economy once again on a growth path.

All of the above requires saying in consideration of the enormous amounts of ink being spilled by economists and pundits about the looming "recession." As usual, they know not what they speak. Recessions signal recovery. This will not be that kind of recession. It won't be simply because it's not reasonable to suggest that what's taking place right now is in a broad sense a realization of individual and corporate error, a cessation of individual and companywide bad habits, and individual/corporate rebuilding of balance sheets.

It's not simply because what we're experiencing is the asphyxiation of economic activity on the local, state and national level. Though the *Wall Street Journal*'s editorial page oddly supports the Fed and federal government as a major capital allocator to businesses wrecked by asphyxiation, the same page makes the correct point that the U.S. economy of March 19th is very different from the one of, say, February 19th. That one was largely free, while this one, per the Journal's editorialists, is the stuff of "command and control."

Translated for those who need translation of the obvious, this won't be a recession. Recessions are yet again painful, but always healthy periods of error realization when free individuals and businesses fix what's wrong.

In 2020, matchlessly foolish politicians are to varying degrees not allowing individuals and businesses to work and produce. Good times didn't bring on this horror show we're being forced to endure; rather this contraction is and will be a consequence of way-too-powerful politicians decreeing the work of all too many illegal.

To be clear, what's ahead is a contraction born of monumental political error. Good history, Benjamin Anderson-style history, will make this screamingly apparent. There was never in 2020 an economic crisis born of a spreading virus; rather a spreading virus proved oxygen for politicians on all levels on the way to them forcing contraction on an economy that, if large and growing larger, would be most capable of slaying the virus.

Indeed, it's fascinating in these times to see even rhetorically-friendly-to-market conservatives calling for a muscular governmental response to what is a political problem. The very central planning that conservatives decry in normal times apparently makes sense during crisis, thus resulting in Kevin Warsh as the spokesman for conservatives lurching to government as their savior.

The joke is on them. It seems they missed the simple truth that government spending is a consequence of private sector economic activity, yet the private sector is presently being suffocated by the very politicians conservatives seek to empower right now. To witness what's happening is to wish it were a bad dream. Except that bad dreams aren't this awful.

Which brings us to the last certain aspect of recessions; this aspect always and everywhere a major driver of the economic recovery that recession signals. During downturns individuals and businesses yet again pull back, they become more careful, they save. And their savings set the stage for a rebound. The problem, in 2020, is that what savings many Americans have will be consumed just to make sure the eviction notices don't come, the lights stay on, that food is around to be eaten.

It's all a reminder that what we're about to endure has nothing to do with recession. Let's please not insult what's happening with a word that has everything to do with recovery. Recessions signal something better on the way. Command and control economies designed by hapless politicians and central bankers signal agonizing economic decline.

WHAT CORONAVIRUS TEACHES US ABOUT HUMAN CONNECTION
BY ALLEN MENDENHALL

March 19, 2020.

"Only connect!" reads the epigraph to E.M. Forster's novel Howards End. That phrase possibly encapsulates Forster's entire philosophy.

It is also contrary to the current commands of our authorities and the mass media: Stay home! Keep inside! Close down! Quarantine! Be afraid! Socially distance! Don't gather in groups!

However prudent they may be under the circumstances, these imperatives seem strange, confusing, and unnatural. Most of us don't like alienating ourselves from others for lengthy periods. In times of trouble, we want to help others. We want to do something. If the coronavirus has harmed our psychology, if it has bothered or disturbed us, it is probably because we feel so helpless and vulnerable in the face of its transmittable power. The only thing we can do is… nothing.

Perhaps there is a silver lining. Absent tangible contact with others, we find communities online and via information technologies. Can't visit your elderly parent or grandparent in the nursing home? Here's a web camera. Can't make that meeting in Boston or Atlanta? No problem: chat on Skype or Zoom or Google. Can't visit the Met? Happily, that opera is live streamed!

None of this would have been possible, let alone conceivable, a century ago. Free markets and the innumerable innovations of countless entrepreneurs have improved our lives and institutions in ways we take for granted. As bad as circumstances seem, they could be much worse.

It is popular in some circles to caricature those who celebrate free markets as cold, utilitarian ideologues promoting a radically technocratic vision of society that is characterized by atomized individuals ruthlessly committed to wealth maximization at the expense of the less fortunate. Nothing could be further from the truth. Markets are about freedom, coordination, cooperation, collaboration, association, peace, commerce, prosperity, and exchange. They bring people together. They incentivize trade and honest dealing over violence and war, and voluntary consent over coercion and compulsion.

As the stock market tumbles and businesses shut down, as we quit spending money on everyday goods and pleasures, as we restrict travel and shutter restaurants and bars, perhaps we will begin to more fully appreciate the beauty and joy that a free economy enables.

I have spent the last week as a visiting scholar at AIER, enjoying the company of kind, hospitable colleagues while living in the grand and elegant Edgewood Estate. In sharp contrast to the coronavirus hysteria and panic I've seen in popular media, life here has been calm, friendly, warm, and studious. We dine together for each meal, maintaining the appropriate distance of course. We help each other clean rooms and wash dishes. We meet for cocktail hour each evening after a long day of rigorous research and writing. On these occasions we discuss our work, seek advice and feedback, exchange information and data, and test our theories and arguments. The ideas we bandy about don't end right then and there. They form the basis of articles and of interviews for television and radio. They find their way onto AIER's website, the traffic for which, this week alone, has hit unprecedented levels.

I have noticed during my time here, gradually and by slow degrees, something far more infectious than coronavirus: ideas. Even in self-imposed isolation, the keen intellects at AIER have managed to reach people across the globe, providing unique perspectives and key economic insights to those who most want and need it. A communicable virus has nothing on communicable ideas. AIER has met a negative force with a positive one that is stronger and more lasting.

As governments close borders and impose curfews, as militaries take to the streets to enforce martial law, as universities cancel in-person classes and companies send their employees home, it is important to remember how formidable, vigorous, and enduring ideas can be. Deirdre McCloskey's seminal trilogy—*Bourgeois Virtues*, *Bourgeois Dignity*, and *Bourgeois Equality*—surveys the places and periods in which culture, shaped by ideas, facilitated human flourishing to an astonishing extent. Rhetoric and the concepts it conveys are, in her account, the vital factors that explain economic growth in the modern era.

Imagine what could be accomplished if we proliferated ideas about freedom and liberty more widely and quickly than any contagious virus could ever spread. One person comes into contact with another, transmitting an idea, which is passed on to yet another, who shares it with friends and family. Before long the idea has captured the minds of hundreds, then thousands, then millions, then billions. The contagion is academic, not pandemic. It is good, not bad. It is transmissible through any communicative network and doesn't require face-to-face proximity for its rapid diffusion.

Only connect!

This morning, over coffee, I watched the sun rise above the rolling hillsides and heard exuberant birds chirping in the trees. I realized, sitting there, taking in the sights and smells and sounds of the coming spring, that this pandemic, like all upheavals, will pass. Exhilarated, I sensed with growing intensity a feeling not unlike what William Wordsworth must have felt when he wrote that "in this moment there is life and food / For future years."

For many, this is undeniably a dark, sad, and scary hour of sorrow and hardship, loss and pain. You may be mourning or suffering. You may be comforting a sick loved one. You may be locked away in your room. But take solace: light always drives out the darkness, and hope springs eternal.

THE US CORONAVIRUS DEATH RATE IS FALLING, AND GERMANY'S MORE SO

BY STEPHEN C. MILLER

March 19, 2020.

As major news outlets like the *New York Times* have updated the number of cases of COVID-19 and confirmed deaths from it, a new trend has emerged: the death rate, measured as the number of deaths divided by the number of cases, is *falling*.[166]

Six days ago, on March 12th, there were 36 deaths caused by the virus in the U.S. out of a total of 1,215 cases.[167] As of this writing on March 18th, there have been 121 deaths out of a total 7,047 cases.

That is a drop in the death rate from 2.96% to 1.72%.

This is encouraging, as the U.S. death rate so far has been substantially lower than in China and even lower than France and the U.K. There has been much talk about policy responses to stem the spread of COVID-19, but school closings and social distancing should mostly affect growth in the number of cases, not the deadliness of the disease itself.

Why would the U.S. death rate fall so much over just a few days? The answer is that as more people are tested for the virus, the death rate falls because it becomes more accurate.

And the most accurate data are likely coming from Germany, which arguably has had better testing than any other country. Germany also has the lowest death rate, at just over 0.1%. If that number sounds

---

166 NYT. 2020. "The Coronavirus Outbreak." *The New York Times*, March 19.

167 Dayen, David. 2020. "Unsanitized: The COVID-19 Daily Report, March 13, 2020." *the American Prospect*, March 13.

familiar, it is roughly the death rate from the 2018-19 flu season in the U.S.

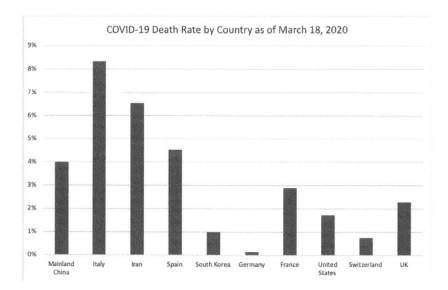

So why is the death rate in Germany so low, and why is it falling in the U.S., exactly? The answer is simple arithmetic. If only people who are hospitalized or very sick get tested, then the denominator—the number of COVID-19 cases—will be biased downward. Those with milder symptoms or no symptoms will not be counted, and the virus will appear more deadly than it really is

For a clear explanation of the illusions created by our incomplete data, and the clarity provided by an accurate denominator, see this from OurWorldinData.[168]

168 Roser, Max, Hannah Ritchie, Esteban Ortiz-Ospina. 2020. See section on 'There are two reasons why the case fatality rate does not reflect the probability of death.' In "Coronavirus Disease (COVID-19)—Statistics and Research." *OurWorldInData.org*, March 19.

This is surely the case in China and Italy, but it is also likely true in France, the U.K., and even in the U.S. currently. But if testing is more widespread and rapid, then officials get a more accurate estimate of the true death rate. It may be true that quicker, more comprehensive testing can reduce the spread of the disease by allowing for more effective quarantines, but again, that should not make the virus less deadly to those who already have it.

In other words, while Germany is a relatively rich, healthy country, there is no reason why its death rate from COVID-19 should be a fraction of what it is in other similarly rich, healthy countries. What differs is measurement. And part of the reason testing was more effective in Germany is that it was decentralized. Independent labs have been doing the testing, without the direction of a central bureaucracy.

A recent *New York Times* article highlights this trend and attributed the lower death rate in Germany to better testing, but by a different mechanism; treatment improves when doctors know what they are dealing with:

> Unlike in other countries, where national laboratories had a monopoly on testing, Germany's distributed system helped doctors to swiftly determine whether suspected cases actually involved the new virus or a common cold, which can have similar symptoms.

It surely helped in Germany, but it is hard to believe that doctors in Seattle or New York treating patients with a fever or cough right now are not erring on the side of caution. What is surely true is that by testing more people more quickly, Germany has much more accurately measured the number of COVID-19 cases, which most countries are under-stating.

Final note: the latest numbers in the US point to a continued drop in the death rate as testing accelerates.[169]

---

169 Worldometer. 2020. "United States Coronavirus." *Worldometer,* March 19.

BEWARE OF PANIC POLICYMAKING
BY VERONIQUE DE RUGY

March 20, 2020.

During this coronavirus pandemic, federal, state and local governments have taken—and are continuing to take—unprecedented measures to combat the epidemic, as well as the recession that will surely soon follow.

People are understandably panicked, and many are willing to indiscriminately turn massive amounts of additional power over to the government. Spending restraints be damned! Any government spending is good spending in times of crisis, apparently as evidenced by the cry for the federal government to send to everyone $1,000 or more alongside an expansion of many safety-net programs.

From the shutdown of the economy to new and boosted transfers to loans to bailouts and handouts, the order of the day is to put as many such policies on the table and not bother to ask if this is the right thing to do.

Calls for caution and accountability or the expression of being concerned with the future financial health of this country are perceived as simplistic, and those who make them are accused of being in denial of the scale of the problem we are facing. Even asking whether these policies would achieve their intended goal—some of them certainly will but others won't—is treated as callous and uncaring behavior. To be wise, on the other hand, is to say yes to every "stimulus package" rushed through even if it means that legislators have no time to read the bills they are voting for.[170]

During emergencies, some reservations about government interventions might be put aside. However, we must nevertheless remind people that blindly putting faith in government interventions is as unwise as refusing to have government act at all during extreme crises.

This fact remains relevant: even in normal times the government supports many bad, irresponsible, and unjust policies, driven in part by perverse incentives. Not the least of these is an imprudent eagerness to please special interests.

In addition, emergencies and the resulting panic only further loosen whatever weak restraints there normally are against government misbehavior and malfunction. The truth is that politicians remain politicians, and most of them don't abandon their misguided ideas because we are in a crisis.

Take, for instance, President Trump's recent executive order to reduce U.S. reliance on foreign-made medical supplies. Driven by the same misguided protectionist spirit that has animated him since he got

---

170 Justin Amash. 2020. "With all due respect, the legislature is supposed to legislate. Every member of Congress needs to participate in the legislative process, not just a few individuals. No more secret bills that we vote on without giving input or reading. If remote sessions are necessary, so be it." *Twitter*, March 16. https://twitter.com/justinamash/status/1239624624855568384?s=20; Justin Amash. 2020. "Technical corrections." Representatives weren't given the official text of the changes and weren't even in town to vote, because House leaders had sent us home. It passed by unanimous consent in a nearly empty chamber." *Twitter*, March 17. https://twitter.com/justinamash/status/1239953883943878656?s=20; Justin Amash. 2020. "House leaders gave us less than 30 minutes to review the revised bill. My staff and I had reviewed prior drafts, and we worked quickly to compare the 110 pages. Upon review, it was clear I couldn't responsibly vote for the bill. Some key provisions appeared unworkable as drafted." *Twitter,* March 14. https://twitter.com/justinamash/status/1238697075606458368.

into office, Trump is pursuing this policy by imposing a mandate to "buy American" even though such costly barriers to the acquisition of health-care products is particularly idiotic during a public health emergency crisis.

This policy is in line with the tariffs he imposed on roughly $5 billion of medical imports from China—that's about 26% of U.S. health-care imports. These tariffs have made it much harder for first responders, healthcare providers, and Americans in general to get facemasks, gloves, and many other health-care products now desperately demanded.

The *WSJ* reports: [171]

> U.S. medical distributors are busy hunting for alternative producers and testing their equipment for interoperability when they should be concentrating on getting supplies to those in need. China, in turn, has diverted its sales to other markets. After President Trump hit Chinese medical suppliers with a 25% tariff in 2018, China's exports to the U.S. dropped by 16%. In some cases, American users had no good alternatives because suppliers must get certified by the Food and Drug Administration, which can take more than two years. U.S. medical-equipment producers have also been plagued by the president's new tariffs on imported components.

Of course, other governments are behaving no better than us. For instance, Switzerland makes ventilators, but due to an EU ban can't get

---

171 Zoellick, Robert B. 2020. "Trump's Tariffs Leave the U.S. Short on Vital Medical Supplies." *The Wall Street Journal*, Opinion, March 18.

component parts from Romania.[172] There are so many other examples of such foolishness that it would take too much space in this column even to list them all.

At home, many politicians are using this crisis to push programs they've long hoped to impose on us. As Majority Whip James Clyburn (D-S.C.) told his colleagues, "This is a tremendous opportunity to restructure things to fit our vision". That way of thinking is visible in the House Democrats' third coronavirus bill. It is full of infrastructure money, expansions of many safety-net programs such as Medicaid and unemployment benefits, paid and sick leave mandates, a $15 minimum wage, and so much more. And, of course, the bill also continues Democrats' crusade against corporations. It does so by imposing restrictions on executive compensation, a prohibition on stock buybacks, and a requirement of profit-sharing.

Republicans, not to be outdone, are trotting out their own pet policies—such as stricter limits on immigration, corporate tax cuts, and others—in the name of dealing with this crisis. Making matters worse, Republicans so far have demonstrated very little willingness to push back on most of the Democrats' demands, and don't seem very preoccupied with adding trillions of dollars to the deficit or worried about the risk that most of the new programs could become permanent fixtures in our lives.

These reasons alone are sufficient to justify deep distrust in politicians' willingness to respond wisely to severe crises. This sad reality is particularly true when the problematic behaviors are not new. As Adam Thierer adeptly explained last week, the U.S. government and

---

172 Siegenthaler, Peter. 2020. "Swiss ventilator company inundated by demand due to Covid-19." *SwissInfo.com*, March 17.

many of its officials—the same who are in charge of responding to this crisis—have badly blotched Coronavirus testing.[173]

At this point, even the media can't ignore the failed response of the precautionary-minded officials at the Centers for Disease Control and Prevention and the Food and Drug Administration—a response that delayed the availability of tests for COVID-19.[174]

Remember, these are the same agencies that spent decades imposing harmful restrictions on our freedom to innovate and produce. That these restrictions are harmful is evidenced by the sudden rush to deregulate that we are seeing right now.

Precisely because we are now more willing to let our guard down we must keep a vigilant eye on all these politicians who are now working hyperactively to "protect" us.

---

173 See article herein entitled "How the US Botched Coronavirus Testing."

174 Raymond, Art. 2020. "Utah company ready to crank out 50K COVID-19 tests per day." *DeseretNews*, March 17; Court, Emma. 2020. "In Coronavirus Testing Ramp-Up, U.S. Called Private Sector in Late." *Bloomberg*, March 17; Whoriskey, Peter, Neena Satija. 2020. "How U.S. coronavirus testing stalled: Flawed tests, red tape and resistance to using the millions of tests produced by the WHO." *The Washington Post*, March 16.; Weaver, Christopher, Betsy McKay & Brianna Abbott. 2020. "America Needed Coronavirus Tests. The Government Failed." *The Wall Street Journal*, March 19.

MEDICAL-SUPPLY NATIONALISM IS DEEPLY HARMFUL, EVEN DEADLY
BY MAX GULKER

March 20, 2020.

The interconnectedness of virtually every person on the planet, more than any other change, defines the modern world. In relatively normal times the meetings of billions of minds have brought prosperity beyond what virtually all our ancestors could comprehend.

That prosperity is hard for anyone to debate, which is likely why economists who are often perplexingly able to disagree on almost any issue, form an almost united front on questions like international trade and immigration. Those same forces have also created confusion and fear that we can't ignore.

That fear and confusion are a core part of what allowed President Donald Trump to win office, in no small part by opposing the near-consensus among economists. In a somewhat cruel twist of fate, the global COVID-19 pandemic that escalates these fears from populist rallying cry to frenzied power grab has happened under his watch.

Given the opportunity, an administration that exploited a turn against modernity all the way to the White House door was sure to reach again for those levers of fear and misunderstanding. Mirroring what appears to be a backslide into authoritarianism around the globe, the past several days have seen the Trump administration put its cynical tariffs-first trade policy into fast forward.

Of the two economists most prominently in the President's corner on trade, former advisor Stephen Moore emerged as an apologist to polite society, able to ruminate on how the President's tariffs would discipline the bad actors in China and allow us to have it both ways with prosperous trade and intoxicating national pride.

Even if Moore was still clocking in at the White House, this unique moment likely still would have fallen into the hands of trade advisor Peter Navarro, perhaps more realistic than Moore in accepting the tension between trade and nationalism, but more than happy to sacrifice the former for the latter.

As confusion and tension from COVID-19 ratchet upward, he's found a button to push in advocating an "America First" approach to medicine and essential hospital supplies.[175] We needn't overthink our response—we must reject this harmful and ugly piece of politics without hesitation.

PARTY OF ONE

Navarro is a truly distinct specimen in the modern economics profession—before Trump's election I was not aware that something called neo-mercantilism existed—it still may not after Navarro retires.[176] Economists on all sides will understand the oddity of a modern take on the idea that the world's nation-states are locked in battle over already-maxed out wealth. Adam Smith slaying the dragon of mercantilism in *The Wealth of Nations* is of course an oversimplification but its status as the origin myth of modern economics underscores how central the shift was from wars over gold to gains from trade.

This all may seem arcane to those who've spent less time buried in economics books, and it may seem like common sense to look out for one's neighbors before the rest of the world. Fortunately Navarro's

---

175 Crilly, Rob. 2020. "'It's about our very national defense': Trump to slash use of foreign medical supplies, Navarro says." *Washington Examiner*, March 11.

176 Wikipedia. 2020. "Peter Navarro." *Wikipedia,* 21 March.

own analysis of the spectre of depending on foreigners for hospital masks provides the perfect teachable moment.

One of the few emerging ideas where feuding camps seem to find consensus is the strain that a large number of cases of COVID-19, even if usually not deadly, could put on the resources of hospitals. Surgical masks have become emblematic of this problem—less protection for the medical professionals that wear them and more prevention of those treating others becoming points of contagion themselves.

Navarro looks into the interconnected modern world that's brought so much prosperity and knowledge, and sees non-Americans who might take our masks. "This is not just about public health and safety. It's about our very national defense." He goes on to explain what we must do in "Trump time," which means really fast:

In terms of tackling the problem, it's a three-pronged Trumpian strategy consistent with everything the president has done—a synergistic combo of 'Buy American,' regulatory streamlining at the FDA and EPA, and competitive advanced manufacturing supremacy through technological innovation.

Perhaps I haven't spent enough time with the literature on international trade, but I assume "competitive advanced manufacturing supremacy," which sounds like the words of an authoritarian propagandist if that authoritarian propagandist was eleven years old, is Navarro's invention.

Navarro correctly worries about a shortage—we do have one now. His solution is to tie a hand behind our back by mandating that all federal agencies, and Navarro hopes contractors too, must Buy American for a list of medical supplies. The reason reveals logic every bit as circular as the old diagrams explaining the mercantilist system—we need to create demand for our new American medical supplies factories.

When there is a shortage of medical supplies, going out of our way to make them more expensive will hurt people. These are also not perishable goods—stockpiling them from efficient sources to be deployed in a future crisis seems like a safer bet than shiny new idle factories waiting to ramp up production when the next virus hits.

Even the rest of the President's trade bureaucracy sees through this nonsense—they've been granting exemptions for medical supplies among the tariffs Trump and others put in place.

Protectionists, or those profiteering from its appeal, inevitably fall back on the aging trope that we might go to war with the rival nation du jour who also might have the factories. That's an increasingly obsolete worst case scenario, but by all means let's discuss it—just not in "Trump time" under pandemic conditions.

SEND NAVARRO PACKING

I've personalized this deep disagreement with Navarro's idea, something I usually try not to do. But libertarians, progressives, plenty of Wall Street conservatives, and likely a surprising number of democratic socialists—groups all more suspicious of each other right now than likely in my whole lifetime—can all reject these unequivocally bad ideas.

International trade, in which the decency and inclusiveness of free markets is impossible to ignore, might give us a moment to ever so briefly exhale and establish that there are limits to our admittedly profound disagreements.

Henry George, the Gilded Age economist who somehow inspired both libertarians and socialists, is worth quoting at length, now more than ever:

Religion and experience alike teach us that the highest good of each is to be sought in the good of others; that the true interests of men are harmonious, not antagonistic; that prosperity is the daughter of goodwill and peace; and that want and destruction follow enmity and strife. The protective theory, on the other hand, implies the opposition of national interests; that the gain of one people is the loss of others; that each must seek its own good by constant efforts to get advantage over others and to prevent others from getting advantage over it.

Maybe we can let the ugliest of responses to a moment of understandable fear draw a couple of lines in the sand even while other seemingly endless debates about our politics and economics push on.

INCARCERATION, MONETIZATION, AND NATIONALIZATION CAN'T PRESERVE OUR HEALTH OR WEALTH
BY RICHARD M. SALSMAN

March 21, 2020.

After only a few months of a quick global spread of the Wuhan China virus ("COVID-19"), evidence is mounting that it won't prove as deadly as first projected; yet there's still a high level of hysteria and an ominous spread of deleterious economic and public health policies, amounting to *incarceration*, *monetization*, and *nationalization*. What's needed instead—if health and wealth are desired—is *deregulation*, *tax relief*, and *capitalism*.

It's good news that some "red tape" has been removed to allow drug makers and health care pros to better (and more freely) do their jobs. That can improve and solve things, but it shouldn't take an emergency for people to have more liberty, and the real problem today is the *reverse*: liberties are being lost out of an irrational obsession with safety and security, with a puerile need for a "social safety net" immunizing us from every change and risk.

This phobia has led Mr. Trump and his team to close borders and declare "war" in peacetime, which means *to declare war against citizens*, even invoking a never-repealed Defense Production Act (1950) that gives the executive branch vast power to commandeer resources, nationalize industries, and impose wage-price controls.

Tragically, bipartisan support exists for this approach. This week the governors of California and New York—each of whom is a Democrat eyeing the prize of a future White House gig—mandated near-complete shutdowns of nearly all socially-productive activity in their regal realms, including "non-essential business." They and other state governors also want to use the National Guard, while mayors of major cities (Los Angeles, New York, etc.) impose curfews and adopt measures that are akin to martial law. Meanwhile, many officials are emptying prisons and refusing to fully enforce laws against shoplifting.

It's well known that one side of the American bipartisan divide (Republican) favors policies reflecting *nationalism* while the other side (Democrat) favors policies reflecting *socialism*.

That's the case here too, in dealing with COVID-19. Sometimes the two sides clash, but we also observe them finding common ground. A *synthesis* of the two, if you know your history, would be *national socialism*. Look it up and see whether it's really something you want or, regardless, whether it's something you'll eventually get.

Initially, according to an influential but catastrophist study from London Imperial College, which was widely promulgated by the World Health Organization (WHO), COVID-19 was estimated to have a global death rate of 3.4% for those eventually infected, peaking in mid-2020. But that high estimate came from a mere hypothetical model based solely on China's early, most intense experience with COVID-19.

Even if the actual, future global death rate of the virus becomes ten times the 0.1% historical death rate for those who contract the common flu each season, it would be 1.0%, or roughly 1/3rd of the 3.4% estimate. Even *The New York Times*, prone to sensationalizing COVID-19 out of political bias, reported recently that "Coronavirus Death Rate in Wuhan is Lower Than Previously Thought."[177]

---

177 Belluck, Pam. 2020. "Coronavirus Death Rate in Wuhan Is Lower than Previously Thought, Study Finds." *The New York Times*, March 19.

Globally, so far, Johns Hopkins University reports 255,305 cases of COVID-19 infections, with 157,510 of those (62%) unresolved, 87,351 (34%) recovered, and 10,444 (4%) ending in death.[178] Many of those who have died were older folks and/or those with pre-existing conditions (diabetes, heart and respiratory diseases, etc.). Very little attention has been paid to the fact that there are many survivors, probably because it's not sensationalist enough; yet epidemiologists say survivors provide valuable data for determining optimal treatment. Most of those who recovered were not spending their prior weeks in self-exile or home hibernation, as public officials now demand; older people are more likely to live alone.

An informative, compelling scientific analysis of COVID-19 was issued recently by Dr. John Ioannidis, professor of medicine, epidemiology and population health, biomedical data science, and statistics at Stanford University, and co-director of its Meta-Research Innovation Center.[179] He contends that the COVID-19 event is a potential "fiasco in the making," because decisions today, public and private alike, are not sufficiently based on reliable evidence or sound science, and the evidence suggests strongly that this is a virus likely to generate far less dire effects than many now believe. For Ioannidis:

> Reasonable estimates for the case fatality ratio [of COVID-19] in the general U.S. population vary from 0.05% to 1%... If 1% of

---

178 Johns Hopkins University. 2020. "Coronavirus COVID-19 Global Cases by the Center for Systems Science and Engineering (CSSE) at Johns Hopkins University (JHU)."

179 Ioannidis, John P.A. 2020. "A fiasco in the making? As the coronavirus pandemic takes hold, we are making decisions without reliable data." *Stat*, March 17.

the U.S. population gets infected (about 3.3 million people), this would translate to about 10,000 deaths. This sounds like a huge number, but it is buried within the noise of the estimate of deaths from "influenza-like illness. If we had not known about a new virus out there, and had not checked individuals with PCR tests, the number of total deaths due to 'influenza-like illness' would not seem unusual this year. At most, we might have casually noted that the flu this season seems to be a bit worse than average. The media coverage would have been less than for an NBA game between the two most indifferent teams.

(See also his paper "Why Most Published Research Findings Are False," cited more than 8,000 in the literature.)[180]

Consider some other recent context: the H1N1 virus (*aka* "swine flu") originated in Mexico in March 2009 and by mid-March of 2010 the U.S. Centers for Disease Control and Prevention (CDC) estimated that 59 million Americans were infected; of that, only 265,000 (0.4%) were hospitalized while 12,000 died. The death rate from H1N1 (0.02%, or total deaths divided by total infected) was *twice* the long-term average death rate of the common flu, but still miniscule.

As of today, the U.S. has 17,962 confirmed cases of COVID-19 and 239 deaths from it, a fatality of 1.3%. Certainly, the case count will rise, perhaps by a lot, but to anything close to 59 million? Unlikely. COVID-19 isn't yet like the H1N1 virus, although it's now 1/3rd as old.

In 2009-10, the media infrequently and quietly covered the "swine flu;" there was no widespread phobia, no government bans on peaceful

---

180 Ioannidis, John P.A. 2005. "Why Most Published Research Findings Are False." *Plos Medicine*, August 30.

assembly, no shutdowns of economic activity, no stock-price crash.

Given the impeachment hysteria of 2018-20 and the partisan motives that drove it, perhaps the main difference between the mild reaction to the more lethal H1NI virus in 2010 and the hyped, heated reaction to the Wuhan China virus in 2020 is the difference between President Obama, who was adored by most of the media, and President Trump, who, we know, is reviled by most of it.

AIER has been an important, sober, and objective source of evidence, analysis, and context for COVID-19, tracking and reporting the vital information which seems lost on the sensationalists in media and the power-seekers in politics.[181] It's also been careful to consider a full context, not just the bio-medical aspects but also the social, economic, financial, and political aspects. It knows we mustn't be myopic.

Other good sources include Johns Hopkins University and Our World in Data.[182] I'm an economist and political scientist, not an epidemiologist or virologist, but I also know that data and models can be manipulated by credentialed ideologies seeking to grind an axe or push a pre-virus agenda.

There's good reason to believe that such manipulation is happening with COVID-19, and even if it is a minor factor, it's a major factor if heavily relied upon by public officials wielding political power and imposing potentially harmful policies on millions of people.

---

181 AIER Staff. 2020. "Vital Information that Is Falling Through the Cracks." *American Institute for Economic Research*, March 20.

182 Johns Hopkins University (2020); Roser, Max, Hannah Ritchie & Esteban Ortiz-Ospina. 2020. "Coronavirus Disease (COVID-19) – Statistics and Research." *Our World in Data*, March 24.

Now let's briefly examine the three main public (and private) policy approaches to the arrival of COVID-19 in America: incarceration, monetization, and nationalization.

INCARCERATION

To "incarcerate" means to imprison people who are guilty and justly convicted of legally criminal acts. That's not quite what's happening now, but it isn't far from the truth either. The policy now spreading nationwide is called "lockdown," a *prison* term; some call it "shelter in place," which seems less harsh, but isn't if it's enforced or its disobedience is penalized. The technique of "house arrest" incarcerates people in their abode and restricts their freedom of movement, but such people nonetheless have been convicted of criminal acts, and if they violate the conditions of their home confinement, they risk more severe imprisonment. Today, in contrast, we're witnessing a *near-universal house arrest of innocents*, of people *presumed* to be guilty (i.e., infected, thus dangerous to others) *unless* they can prove their innocence, which is a direct contravention of fair jurisprudence, Moreover, this is happening without much complaint, opposition or civil disobedience.

A nationwide government mandate of *near-universal house arrest* is not only a brazen assault on civil liberties, but also on economic liberties, for it violates the freedom to peaceably assemble, to associate, to produce in groups at firms, to interact, exchange, trade, profit, and prosper. It undermines the confidence people might have in the intelligence, integrity, and poise of their leaders; it makes the future more difficult to predict, thus freezing activity, and *more* difficult even than predicting the future path of the familiar, bell-shaped disease curve. As such, it erodes the preservation of both wealth and health, not to mention that it sabotages people's natural and healthy desire to socialize, entertain, recreate and "refuel." It's certainly no solution to the problem of COVID-19.

There is some common sense, of course, in identifying, testing, and treating the infected, if necessary even to declare publicly that people will be held liable if they know they're sick and yet knowingly interact with and jeopardize the health and life of others. Quarantines are justified if selective and fact-based, even for restricting entry from those arriving from suspect areas; but to *indiscriminately quarantine everyone* is unjust, impractical, and destructive. For COVID-19 already, death rates are low and recoveries high, so there's good evidence that, like prior viruses, human interaction (not "social distancing") may *help us* develop antibodies and immunities, all of which is lost if we are forcibly confined to homes.

Is there also no possible manifestation here of the law of unintended consequences? Consider only the possible viral effects of compelling millions of college students, just back from intensely congregating during "spring break," to board thousands of airplanes to go home and intermingle with parents and grandparents. The young can carry a virus with low infection rates, but the elderly are highly vulnerable; COVID-19 death rates are high in Italy partly because of its socialized medicine (which limits the system's capacity, quality and responsiveness) but also because it has one of the world's oldest populations.

MONETIZATION

Monetization, another policy adopted in the wake of the arrival of COVID-19 entails the U.S. government (the Fed, Treasury, and various agencies) printing, borrowing, and spending vast sums of money—$1-2 trillion at latest count—on firms lacking sufficient revenues only because employees and customers were told to vacate and hibernate, and on citizens who've been dismissed from jobs and now do little or nothing at home (its untrue that "everyone can work from home" or that those doing so work as productively).

Since when does the mere creation of money—especially unbacked, inconvertible fiat money—create employment, wealth or prosperity? It doesn't. It can't. It only means that real wealth is being redistributed arbitrarily, not created freely and objectively. Wealth, we should all know by now, isn't multiplied by dividing it, nor by rearranging it via monetary manipulations. In fact, these manipulations make production less likely, because the bias of issuance, including through public lending, is towards subsidizing and rewarding the illiquid and/ or insolvent, at the expense of betters. Money *represents* wealth; it is not *itself* wealth. Is this so difficult to grasp?

Consider also the policy of zero interest rates, now almost universally adopted by major central banks; everyone seems convinced that this should "stimulate" the economy by stimulating borrowing; ignored is the supply side of credit markets, and the lack of incentive for creditors to lend when they aren't compensated. Is this difficult to grasp? Moreover, should firms and people borrow more when they're shut down and making less or no money? The Keynesians love the zero-interest-rate policy, which is a major reason we're seeing it adopted; they say it entails a welcome "euthanasia of the *rentier*" (the despised lender); now watch, as it also euthanizes the economy and credit markets.

Likewise, issuing more public debt and placing it on an already-indebted economy compelled to produce less is irresponsible and self-defeating. More leverage means more debt relative to equity or net worth; more leverage is certainly *not* more wealth. Is this difficult to grasp? There is also no so-called "government spending multiplier," despite what Keynesians like Paul Krugman have been claiming and preaching for decades. There's no magic wand whereby a dollar spent by politicians in the public sector creates wealth relative to what producers achieve in the private sector by spending the same dollar. Such mystical powers "exist" only in Potterism, not in capitalism (or reality).

Not only does the issuance of fake money and debt create no real wealth, but those who believe it does so also seem to believe that wealth creation itself is a "problem" to be "solved" by curbing or stopping it. This is the Keynesian myth that economic recessions reflect "deficient demand," which allegedly results from previous "overproduction."

So-called "general glut theorists" have been around for centuries, at least since the non-scientific Reverend Malthus (in the late 1700s) and persists to this day despite repeated refutations (by J.B. Say, Frederic Bastiat, Henry Hazlitt, etc.).[183] It's incredible that anyone today would still believe it, especially in today's context; is the arrival of COVID-19 proof that the world previously "overproduced?"

Yet the U.S. Secretary of Energy recently said that he and Mr. Trump were trying to *reduce oil output*, to boost the oil price. Similar policies, adopted in the early 1930s, transformed a recession into a multi-year Great Depression. Most notably, FDR's New Deal AAA (Agricultural Adjustment Administration) paid farmers *not* to produce, even to burn crops, slaughter farm animals, and pour milk down drains—all to boost agriculture prices and keep the supply-side in business. Meanwhile the demand side of the market, the millions of consumers suffering

183 Salsman, Richard M. 2020. "Say's Law versus Keynesian Economics." *American Institute for Economic Research*, February 9.

in bread lines and soup kitchens, faced mass unemployment (which peaked at 25% in 1933), due to a similar Keynesian scheme of keeping prices (wage rates) artificially high.

NATIONALIZATION

Finally, consider the growing calls for the U.S. government to *nationalize* and/or control American businesses, in whole or part, allegedly to fight COVID-19. This is the hoped-for policy of the likes of avowed anti-capitalists Bernie Sanders and Elizabeth Warren, but now Mr. Trump also wants to wield the power. He's perfectly comfortable with it.

This week Mr. Trump invoked the Defense Production Act (1950), not to fight a war but to fight a virus, which is odd, because virus fighting should be the job of chemists, virologists, and epidemiologists.

What motivates this? The DPA gives the U.S. executive branch near-limitless power to impose wage-price controls, commandeer private resources, and nationalize firms and industries. The DPA neither cures a virus nor boosts investor confidence. It doesn't create wealth but destroys it. It says when times are tough, policy should be based on emotion, coercion, and socialism, not on reason, incentives, and capitalism. President Truman used the DPA, but it didn't help the U.S. win the Korean War.

The scheme of government in the U.S. taking shares or board seats in companies sometimes relates only to the policy of publicly subsidizing or bailing them out. But the subsidies and bailouts are *themselves* unjustified; two wrongs don't make a right. Is this so difficult to grasp?

Other people argue that the subsidies and bailouts are warranted if the illiquidity, insolvency and failures are due mainly to the government's policy of mandating closures. But that policy is itself unjustified;

again, two wrongs don't make a right. We also hear that firms receiving government financial aid or loans shouldn't be free to pay executives as they wish, nor be free to pay their shareholders, whether by dividends or share buybacks.

Yes, being a creditor or owner of a firm implies some control, but government bailouts, as mentioned, are unjustified, as is the policy of government ownership, and so also is the policy of decreeing how a firm shall be managed or how its executives and shareholders should be paid. Is this difficult to grasp?

When these three policies take hold, production plummets, and the full carnage is finally tallied, just watch as the culprits are again held blameless—indeed, extolled, as they were in 2008-09, as they insist (as they did then) that things would have been *worse* had their policies not been adopted.

800 MEDICAL SPECIALISTS CAUTION AGAINST DRACONIAN MEASURES
BY EDWARD P. STRINGHAM

March 24, 2020

If you depend only on mass media during this crisis, one's perspective can become distorted. You might gain the impression that the whole world agrees that a full lockdown of life itself is the only way to control the spread of Coronavirus and minimize the fatalities. But this doesn't take into account what actual medical professionals are saying right now.

Hundreds of professors associated with Yale University organized a letter with signatures[184] to send to the White House. It was signed by 800 credentialed professionals largely from the fields of epidemiology and medicine. It is not what I would call a free-market treatise, to be sure, and I do not agree with parts of it.

Still, it takes us in a different direction, and a much more libertarian one, than the one in which governments are taking us. The letter warns that the crackdowns, shutdowns, travel restrictions, sweeping closures, and work restrictions could be counterproductive and not produce the results people hope for. This echoes the concern expressed by Stanford epidemiologist John Ioannidis and his recently published work[185] that

---

184 (2020, March 2) Achieving A Fair and Effective COVID-19 Response: An Open Letter to Vice-President Mike Pence, and Other Federal, State and Local Leaders from Public Health and Legal Experts in the United States. Yale Global Health Justice Partnership.

185 Ioannidis, John P. A. 2020. "Coronavirus disease 2019: the harms of exaggerated information and non-evidence-based measures." *European Journal of Clinical Investigation*, March 19.

warns that we are taking extreme measures with low-quality information with little interest in costs.

And where the letter worries about the loss of public services, I would add the worry of the loss of essential economic services. I will quote large sections of this letter. My main message here is as follows. If you worry that the coercive measures government is using and proposing go way too far, you are not alone: many in the mainstream of the medical profession agree with you.

> **Mandatory quarantine, regional lockdowns, and travel bans have been used to address the risk of COVID-19 in the US and abroad. But they are difficult to implement, can undermine public trust, have large societal costs and, importantly, disproportionately affect the most vulnerable segments in our communities.** Such measures can be effective only under specific circumstances. All such measures must be guided by science, with appropriate protection of the rights of those impacted. Infringements on liberties need to be proportional to the risk presented by those affected, scientifically sound, transparent to the public, least restrictive means to protect public health, and regularly revisited to ensure that they are still needed as the epidemic evolves.

> **Voluntary self-isolation measures are more likely to induce cooperation and protect public trust than coercive measures, and are more likely to prevent attempts to avoid contact with the healthcare system.** For mandatory quarantines to be effective and therefore scientifically and legally justified, three main criteria must be satisfied: 1) the disease has to be transmissible

in its presymptomatic or early symptomatic stages; 2) those who may have been exposed to COVID-19 must be able to be efficiently and effectively identified; and 3) those people must comply with the conditions of quarantine. There is evidence that COVID-19 is transmitted in its pre-symptomatic or early symptomatic stages. However, the contribution of infected individuals in their pre-symptomatic or early symptomatic stages to overall transmission is unknown. Efficiently identifying those exposed will be increasingly difficult as community transmission of the virus becomes more widespread, making quarantine a less plausible measure as community spread proceeds. Whether individuals can comply will be determined by the degree of support provided, particularly for low-wage workers and other vulnerable communities. While quarantines are in effect in many places already, their continuing and new use by federal, state or local officials requires real-time assessment and evaluation to justify them as the science and the outbreak evolve, through a transparent, open decision making process including external scientific and legal experts.

It will also be imperative not to impose inhumane or discriminatory conditions, as occurred on the Diamond Princess cruise ship, where passengers were quarantined to protect the population on land but were isolated in a high transmission setting.

Government and employers must recognize that low-wage, gig-economy, and non-salaried workers who are unable to work because of quarantine or movement restrictions or other disruptions to the economy and public life face extraordinary challenges. They may find it impossible to meet their basic needs, or those of their family.

Individuals must be empowered to understand and act upon their rights. Information should be provided on the justification of any mandatory restrictions as well as how and where to appeal such decisions. They should be afforded procedural due process, including universal access to legal counsel, to ensure their claims of discrimination or of hazardous conditions associated with their confinement are adjudicated.

The effectiveness of regional lockdowns and travel bans depends on many variables, and also decreases in the later stages of an outbreak. Though the evidence is preliminary, a recent modeling study suggests that in China these measures may have mitigated but not contained the spread of the COVID-19 epidemic, delaying it locally by a few days, while having a more marked, though still modest, effect at the international scale, particularly if not combined with measures that achieved at least 50% reduction of transmission in the community. Travel restrictions also cause known harms, such as the disruption of supply chains for essential commodities. The authors of a recent review of research on the subject concluded that "the effectiveness of travel bans is mostly unknown" and "when assessing the need for, and validity of, a travel ban, given the limited evidence, it's important to ask if it is the least restrictive measure that still protects the public's health, and even if it is, we should be asking that question repeatedly, and often.

Whether or not one is fully on board with economic liberalism[186], this letter reveals that serious health scholars are not on board with many of the draconian command-and-control measures on the table. Are people in the White House getting the message? I hope so.

---

186 Stringham, Edward A. 2019. *Private Governance: Creating Order in Economic and Social Life*. Published by Oxford University Press: New York, NY.

LEAVING PEOPLE ALONE IS THE BEST WAY TO BEAT THE CORONAVIRUS
BY RICHARD M. EBELING

March 23, 2020.

The world has rapidly moved into a seemingly aggressive paternalistic planning mode in the face of the coronavirus crisis. Many voices are heard to say that personal and economic liberties must be restricted or even temporarily banned. At the same time, many of those same voices are saying that at a moment like this government spending, for all intents and purposes, has no limit. Welcome to the world of a really, much bigger government.

Over the last two weeks, municipal and state governments in places like California, New York, New Jersey, Connecticut, Pennsylvania, and Illinois, to name just a few that the media has particularly publicized, have ordered the virtual shutting down of huge parts of the economy under their respective jurisdictions. They have commanded entire populations of tens of millions of people to not leave their homes other than for a small handful of reasons such as getting medical treatment or food shopping under penalty of a fine or worse.

Millions of people in manufacturing and especially the service sectors of the market have been or are in the process of being thrown out of work because the enterprises in which they are employed have been ordered to close their doors or narrowly reduce the type of business they do until further notice, again subject to legal penalty.

WAR POWERS, BUDGET BUSTING, AND MONETARY EASE

At the federal level, the president of the United States has declared a "national emergency in the fight against the Coronavirus. He has activated a Korean War-era piece of legislation called the Defense Production Act that enables the chief executive to commandeer enterprises and, indeed, entire industries, and compel and direct what those businesses will produce and how and in what quantities to meet the needs of combating the "enemy" threatening the American people. Indeed, at a press conference, President Donald Trump even called himself a "war president."

Reports have appeared warning that the Department of Justice has approached members of Congress to have authority, with a senior judge's approval, to detain individuals indefinitely in declared national emergencies such as the current coronavirus crisis, along with a number of other serious exemptions from respecting a detained person's Constitutional rights and civil liberties.[187]

On the budgetary side, all accounts suggest that the next spending bill coming out of Congress and heading for the president's desk will be in an amount of over $2 trillion, or approximately 10 percent of the U.S. Gross Domestic Product. It contains a grab bag of spending, including sending every American a check from Uncle Sam for up to $1,500 and followed by another check in the same amount later in the spring. Multibillion-dollar bailouts would go to the major airlines and the travel industry to tide them over until large numbers of people start flying and vacationing again.

Loans and guarantees will be extended in, as yet, undefined ways and amounts to small and retail businesses forced to close their establishments due to governmental decrees preventing customers from entering and using their facilities. The Secretary of the Treasury has

---

187 Swan, Betsy Woodruff. 2020. "DOJ seeks new emergency powers amid coronavirus pandemic." *Politico*, March 21.

referred to the federal government having a possible $4 trillion line of credit to extend to businesses adversely affected by the supply-restricting commands imposed by Washington, D.C. or the state governments.

At the same time, America's central bank, the Federal Reserve, has promised easy and available lines of credit for financial institutions and others to help them stay in business and supply the means for borrowers and investors to pay their bills and meet their payrolls in the face of falling or stalled production and sales resulting from those government edicts to stop what they are doing and sending their workers home for self-quarantining and social distancing.

THE NEW COMMAND AND CONTROL ECONOMY

"Social distancing" is the new official language for government telling people not to interact with others at work, or in the common areas of everyday life, or even at home. What it amounts to is the government telling people where, with whom, and when they may associate in close proximity with others for mutually beneficial trades or for various forms of family activities and social comradery and entertainment.

Suppose that the federal government in close collaboration with state governments were to introduce such draconian coercive controls and commands on the American people at any time other than like the present one, when many in the country have become wrapped up in fear and near hysteria over the threat of the coronavirus. I think it is likely that many would wonder if some type of political coup d'état was not in the process of transforming the American Republic into a near totalitarian state and planned economy.

What other conclusions could be drawn when personal freedom and civil liberties were being trampled upon, when the freedom of association both inside and outside the marketplace was being straightjacketed, and private property rights and free enterprise were, respectively, abridged and placed under government direction and dictate?

Because of the concerns surrounding the life and death impact of the coronavirus, the vast majority of the population in the United States (and in all other countries affected by the virus, as well, such as in Europe), acquiesce and support the government telling them what to do in their everyday life, including how to do it.

In addition, the imposition of this system of social authoritarianism is happily pursued as a bipartisan exercise by politicians in expanding the powers and reach of the government at all its levels. At the same time, members of both major political parties never lose sight that in a presidential election year they are playing to the voters in both vigorously seeming to be doing "something" and vastly enlarging the dollars to be eaten up at the government trough by the various groups they normally pander to and which are now suffering due to those new command and control policies they are jointly imposing on the country.

ANY NEW NORMALCY WILL NOT BE THE OLD NORMAL

At some point, as yet not fully determined or predictable, the Coronavirus crisis will come to its end. Many will have been infected by the virus and will have suffered anything from non-existent symptoms to serious illness that has required hospitalization. And, tragically, a certain number who have come down with the virus will succumb to its effects and pass away, especially those in the later years of life who have a variety of pre-conditions that weaken their immune systems to better ward off the viral invader.

The world, including the United States, will attempt to return to some kind of "normal," though what normal means at that time will not be independent of all that has occurred in the interim between the first appearance of the virus and its disappearance, either from "natural" causes or by medical advances in the form of a successful inoculation.

But what most likely will be one of the lingering legacies of the coronavirus crisis will be the presumption that governments not only must take the lead, with all the accompanying power and controls to face and fight a future pandemic, but that it is the duty of every citizen in such situations to do what the political authorities in elected office or appointed in the appropriate bureaucratic offices tell them to do.

FUTURE RECRIMINATIONS WILL LIKELY CALL FOR MORE GOVERNMENT

No doubt, if there are any criticisms and recriminations about who and how things were handled—and they are already in play, given that it is an election year—the corridors of debate most likely will be confined to discussions of the personalities who had been in charge, and the failure on their part to be as farsighted and forthright in implementing various policies as then seem "obvious" after the fact. In other words, discussions will revolve around how better to do the command and control system the next time, especially since the residues of the command and control system introduced during the coronavirus crisis will still be on the books or will still be in effect as a "readiness" for that next time.

Already in the pages of *The Nation* (March 20, 2020), it is decried that too many, including Democrats like Joe Biden, were penny-pinchers in wanting to restrict spending and contain government deficits.[188] The author insists, "When faced with the genuine prospect of annihilation, the only adequate response is to do whatever it takes to prevent it. For the United States government, that means not asking, 'How will

---

188 Grey, Rohan. 2020. "We Can Afford to Beat This Crisis." *The Nation*, March 20.

we find the money'? but instead, 'How will we find (and mobilize) the necessary real resources'?"

Oh, and just as urgent and categorical is finding the money and mobilizing the needed real resources, the author says, to do away with fossil fuels, institute the Green New Deal, assuring everyone "the right to a well-paying job" and "creating the public goods that are available for free to everyone." If we could gather the needed money and organize the required resources to defeat the coronavirus, then surely we can do the same to solve problems x, y, and z, as well as… If only we do so, we will be well on the road to collectivist Utopia.

And others, especially on "the left," also condescendingly smirk that there are no libertarians in a pandemic, as it is pointed out that a Republican administration has turned to government "activism" to fight the virus, thus confirming that the days of market fundamentalism and laissez-faire have reached their end (under the ignorant assumption, of course, that America has had a real free market at any time over the last hundred years).[189]

The Republicans have been doing all in their power to confirm this view of "progressives" by working day and night to bring to the desk of the president that $2 trillion giveaway in the name of overcoming the economic tailspin the government's own policies have produced at the federal and state levels.

SO, WHAT SHOULD GOVERNMENT DO? VERY LITTLE

Now, at this point, it would not be unreasonable for a reader to wonder: So, if the turn toward a system of command and control is not the

---

189 Nicholas, Peter. 2020. "There Are No Libertarians in an Epidemic." *The Atlantic*, March 10.

solution, what should government have done and be doing, when confronted by the coronavirus, given the health risk? Surely the answer could not and cannot be, "Nothing," can it?

My answer, for whatever it may be worth, is that is exactly right: Government should be doing little or next to nothing. The problem is a social and medical one, and not a political one. The best methods and avenues for people, as individuals and as members of groups and participants in society as a whole, to discover and apply that which would be best to deal with a pandemic of this sort is to leave it to the institutions of voluntary civil society and the competitive, profit-directed forces of supply and demand.

The classical liberal conception of the purpose and function of government is to protect the individual lives, liberty and honestly acquired property of the citizens under its jurisdiction. This includes an impartial and equal rule of law. Anything that goes beyond these duties and responsibilities must by necessity involve an encroachment of political power over the actions and decision-making of the free individual.

FREE MEN MAKE THEIR OWN CHOICES, FOR GOOD OR ILL

It is one person claiming the authority over another about how they should live, what they may do, with whom they may interact and for what purpose and under what terms. Whether it is a tyrant who has established his political authority through violent means or whether those claiming that power to tell others how to live their lives are holding their political authority based on a democratic election, it remains, nonetheless, some people commanding the actions and interactions of others who may not voluntarily agree with or consent to what they are being told to do.

But it's "science," or "sound medical findings," to which the individual is being made to conform! It's for his own good, in the face of either that person's ignorance or lack of will and willingness to do what is "really right" for them in a particular instance.

References to "science" and "sound medical findings" as an unchallengeable benchmark of justifiable coercion often sounds amusingly innocent and naïve when looked at from the perspective years or decades later; when science and medicine have advanced much further and we can smilingly look back on what people thought was the "right thing to do," in that earlier and less informed time.

No doubt that is how some of our "science" and medical knowledge will be viewed at some later time in the future. It is the way we look at someone in the 1800s, for instance, who declared with dogmatic certainty on some scientific or social matter, "But, my dear fellow, this is the 19th century!" implying that the state of knowledge was so advanced that the notion of anyone questioning or challenging it is absurd. Our amusement comes from thinking how uninformed and "primitive" their thinking seems to be compared to our far more advanced knowledge and understanding in the 21st century.

THE MORALITY OF LIBERTY REQUIRES NON-INTERFERENCE

Even if someone is absolutely right about the danger from another's actions concerning himself, it would still be wrong to stop his conduct from the perspective of recognizing and respecting his right to live his life as he chooses. If you see your neighbor sprinkling a bit of arsenic on his food, and he continues to do so after you have forthrightly and clearly expressed to him the potential health dangers, either because he does not believe you, or he's willing to run the risk because he likes the taste, or because he wants to commit suicide, you do not have the right to interfere with his actions.

You may reason, argue, plead, and admonish, but a free man may not be interfered with, no matter how frustrating, ignorant, or contrary to reason and science you may consider his conduct to be. Once we open that door, the way is opened for any number of seemingly reasonable and unreasonable demands to dictate and determine how others may live. That some get imposed while others do not, once the premise is accepted, is merely a matter of the prejudices and presumptions of public opinion at a moment in time. Today's "absurd" regulation becomes tomorrow's essential political intervention for the good of others, with no logical end to which that premise may be applied.

This may be all well and good, but individuals interact with others, and their actions, especially when it concerns a deadly and contagious virus like the corona one, can and will infringe and impinge on the lives and well-being of others. People interact in two types of "social spaces;" those that are in the domain of private property and market exchange, and those that are in common areas, with the latter potentially creating problems known as "the tragedy of the commons."

THE ARENA OF PROPERTY, PRICES, AND MARKETS

In the realm of private property, owners can set and the transactors may agree upon the terms and conditions under which they voluntarily interact and associate. For instance, in the workplace those on the shop floor have to wear protective goggles, or fire-resistant types of clothing, or must have special training in the use of various tools and instruments used in the production processes of the enterprise.

People negotiate and agree to the type of work to be done, the wages to be earned, the hours of normal employment, the demeanor and deportment expected of each toward other members in the workforce and customers of the business. Special or unusual or irregular circumstances and situations that may arise may be agreed to ahead of time or dealt with as they arise within the enterprise.

Everything mentioned in the preceding paragraph may differ in specific forms and details among firms and enterprises to suit the particulars of the workplace in question. Patterns of conduct in the private marketplace of work and sales reflect the difference in time and place and purpose. There are as many nuanced rules, procedures and practices as the circumstances that market supply and demand warrant at a moment in time and over time in similar and changing conditions.

What is produced how it is produced, where it is produced, and for whom it is produced is guided and determined by the structure of market prices for both final, finished consumer goods and for the factors of production (land, labor, capital) that are used in various complementary and substitutable ways, under the directing vision of entrepreneurs, enterprisers, and businessmen concerning the shape of consumer demands to come.

Supplies are adapted, coordinated and brought into a balance with the demands of those who wish and are able to buy the goods and services potentially brought to market. Changes in the pattern of consumer demands and shifts in the availability and discovered uses of the means of production constantly and continuously result in processes and periods of adjustment to the new circumstances. Everything, it needs to be remembered, takes time to fully and correctly adapt, even with the best intentions and thoughtful expectations, in trying to correctly anticipate the unexpected and the not completely knowable.

What is brought to bear in all of this is the knowledge, experience, informed judgements, and insightful hunches of all the individual participants of the entire global system of division of labor in the worldwide marketplace of goods and ideas. If, as the saying goes, two heads are better than one, then surely 7.7 billion heads are better than all of the best minds of the relative handful of those in government who would presume to know how to "get things done" in better and more balanced ways than when all those billions of minds are set to work through the motive of profit and the avoidance of loss in attempting to improve one's own circumstances.

PERSONAL CHOICES AND THE TRAGEDY OF THE COMMONS

The tragedy of the commons refers to those areas of social life that have not come under the full orbit of private property and market-based decision-making. These are areas that, as they say, belong to everyone and therefore to no one. It is pointed out, for instance, that a common pasture openly accessible to all will likely be over-grazed as each herdsman tries to get as much out of its use as he can; or a common river to which all have access may be polluted by some (or all) due to no restraint on how and for what the common waterway may be used in the pursuit of private purposes. Most of us have experienced irritation and inconvenience from the trash left by others on "public beaches" to which all in the community have entrance with no personal cost or penalty for not policing the garbage they left behind.

The common areas lack the constraints and incentives that influence people's behavior in using and managing what is privately theirs, with the benefits and the costs of the actions mostly falling upon those private owners from either wise or thoughtless decision-making. Many, if not most, of the environmental problems often experienced in society can be traced back to areas of social interactive life in which private property rights have not been carefully delineated, recognized and secured by custom and law. In other words, they are generally found in those areas in any society in which there is equal access and use under "social communism." It creates those instances usually called "negative externalities."

What does all this have to do with the coronavirus crisis and the role of government in society? The common problem arising from a communicable disease like the coronavirus is that it inescapably spreads from interpersonal actions that occur in relatively close proximity. But this is life; we cannot completely get away from participating in the constant and numerous forms of human association, from which come all the benefits that we share in our modern society.

Someone sneezes or coughs near us; we touch something where another hand has recently been; we "rub shoulders" in crowded spaces; and we naturally and unintentionally touch others, whether the latter is a handshake, or a pat on the back, or a kiss on the cheek.

A by-product of our natural "touchy-feely-ness" is transmission of such things as the flu, which in various strains reappears each year. During the 2017-2018 flu season there were 45 million cases in the United States, 810,000 of which required hospitalization; while 61,000 people died that season from the flu. So far in the 2019-2020 season, which runs from October to May, there have been 38 million cases of flu in the U.S., with 400,000 hospitalizations, and 25,000 deaths, with still two and a half months to go in the current flu season.

People could be "socially distancing" themselves more, going shopping less frequently, avoiding more social and business activities and events during flu season, and stop touching and kissing others as much as we do. But most of us choose not to be as cautious and careful as we, hypothetically, could be.

We all know in the back of our minds the risk and uncertainty of whether we will be one of the numbers in that statistic. But as the saying goes "You buys your ticket, and you takes your chances," in the public and common arena of social interaction. And we do not expect or decry a failure of government to get in our individual ways in making these decisions.

GOVERNMENT'S ONE-SIZE-FITS-ALL

Are there particular uncertainties with this new Coronavirus? Yes, according to all the scientific and medical experts. Does this call for heightened care and concern in what we do and how we do it? Most certainly. But, the experts have also been able to tell us that, so far, the young seem to be more asymptomatic, the middle age ranges seem to get it, with many of the usual or other flu-like symptoms, but for the large majority in this group it will pass after a period of discomfort and inconvenience, as with the strains of many other flus. The "at risk" are those 60 and especially 70 or older, and particularly if they have any number of preconditions that have or may weaken their immune system.

So how shall we manage the inescapable "commons areas" of everyday life where we are in close proximity with others in many if not most of the things we usually do? One method is the one our command and control government central planners have been imposing. In a typical "one-size-fits-all" approach, local and state governments have shut down entire sectors of the economy, especially the service and entertainment and related business enterprises.

They have been ordered under legal penalty to stay home, to not go out except for those necessities government says you may go out for, and to stay away from workplaces unless they are "essential" employments as the government defines them. Because everyone could be a potential carrier and recipient of the virus, all will be confined within the one corridor of permitted activities as determined by those in political authority.

This societal straitjacket of economic stoppage and slowdown—singularly due to the compulsory command of politicians and bureaucrats—is starting to wreak havoc on the livelihoods and investments of tens of millions of people. It may have been the case that the history of monetary and fiscal policy over the last ten years strongly suggested that a new economic downturn was going to happen sometime in the future.

But it is clear that this slowdown and likely recession is not due to the usual pattern of the business cycle. This has been induced by government telling large numbers of businesses and workers in society to stop working, stop selling, shut down or more narrowly confine how you do your business.

LETTING INDIVIDUALS CHOOSE THEIR ACTIONS IN THE COMMONS AREA

What, in my view, should have been, and can still be done in terms of an "answer" to the health tragedy of the human commons? Those in the medical and biological fields especially knowledgeable about and doing research in virology should share and explain to their fellow citizens the nature, properties and particular dangers from this coronavirus, as is best understood in an evolving situation. And they should, as they have been, recommend the wisest courses of personal and social actions to avoid or at least minimize the likelihood of catching the virus and passing it on to others

At this point, everything else should be left up to the decisions and judgments of the individual members of the society. Will everyone act "rationally" or "reasonably" as "experts" and normal common sense suggests they should? No. We have seen this with news videos of college students and others congregating in large numbers on beaches in

America and Australia, and when asked why, some sound like infantile knuckleheads who say they are bored and "Just want to get drunk and party, man." Is there any meaning to a negative IQ?

But rather than blanketly shutting down these common areas, like the public beaches, or walkways and thoroughfares, just let them alone. As with any tragedy of the commons situation, others will and should have the liberty to adapt and adjust to the actions of these others as best they find it prudent or necessary, given their own situations and circumstances, and personal health concerns.

Let people decide these things for themselves based on their own risk averseness and concerns for not coming down ill and for not infecting others if they come into contact with a carrier. Those in the most susceptible categories of likely danger would and should adapt as they find and think best.

Not everyone over 60 or 70 has a precondition or will die from the virus if they catch it. Those in this age group should be the ones most careful in planning and designing their interactions with others, particularly staying away from the grandchild or great-grandchild who fits into that knucklehead group.

I might mention that some Americans still have, in this context, a healthy Thoreauvian spirit of civil disobedience. Not far from where I live in Mount Pleasant, South Carolina there is a delightful and heavily wooded county park with numerous winding paths perfect for going for a stroll, walking the dog, or for a bicycle ride or a jog.

The county government may have categorically declared all such parks closed until the end of the coronavirus crisis, but a good number of people went over or around the locked gates and enjoyed a warm and blue-skied weekend in this common area, in spite of what the local government dictated. People were in a good mood, highly friendly and bantering back and forth over the situation, and keeping their six feet apart. The voluntary associations of civil society peacefully and intelligently at work in the midst of an infectious virus crisis.

LEAVING PRIVATE ENTERPRISE FREE TO MEET PEOPLES' DEMANDS

What about the private sector of business and industry in the common social space? This, too, government should leave free and unimpeded. In the face of all the publicized short supplies of a variety of goods, including toilet paper and hand sanitizers, new shipments arrive in many places within a day or two—or at least this will continue to do so for as long as state and local governments do not stop these manufacturers from continuing to produce and gear up a greater supply to meet the increased panic-induced demand.

In spite of all the typical attacks on business and profit-making and the "evil" of higher prices for especially scarce goods at this time of fear and concern, it is the private enterprise system that has the institutions and possesses the incentives to make it advantageous and profitably worthwhile to not only "deliver the goods" on the regular and daily basis that we all so very much take for granted, but to meet unusual and extraordinary circumstances such as the present. The value of the competitive market is that it sets those multitudes of minds to work to devise ways to rapidly and effectively get the goods that people now need and want more of than in the usual patterns of events. Changing relative prices reflect greater and lesser demand and supply changes sets in motion adaptations and adjustments to the new circumstances with greater speed and flexibility than any top-down command and control system of government can possibly oversee and manage.

Prices are a signaling system, a vast and interconnected system of human communication that gives the necessary information to those who need to know, so they may utilize their special knowledge and skills and abilities in their localized times and places to rebalance and re-coordinate how and what they do to meet the changed demands of others as quickly as can be done.

It has been the monopoly decision-making and permission process of the Pure Food and Drug Administration (FDA) and the Centers for Disease Control (CDC) that has delayed developing new and improved testing techniques to deal with the coronavirus, as well as impeded revving up the manufacture of testing equipment and related materials and products.

After weeks of delays in not wanting to loosen or give up their command and control over these things, the FDA and the CDC relented and the private sector was partly given greater freedom to produce, develop and supply what has been most urgently needed. As a result, more of these goods soon will be on their way to where they are wanted.

ALLOWING PEOPLE TO WEIGH THE TRADE-OFFS

But what about workplace health and safety in the face of the coronavirus? The people and not a host of politicians and bureaucrats should determine how and what to do to maintain the efforts and energies of production. Employers and employees should be allowed to decide among themselves the best courses of action, in conjunction with the customers' preferences.

In spite of what the writer for *The Nation* magazine may have said, the world and everyone in it is not facing "annihilation." Humanity will not perish, human life will recover and go on, and as with all other similar natural tragedies, efforts will be made to minimize the human loss, but some will succumb, just as is the case with the usual flu every year.

There are always trade-offs, and personal costs and benefits. If there are some commodities in intensely greater demand, with profits to be made employers can offer time-and-a-half, or double—even triple—pay to compensate for the riskier work environment. Some workers will prefer to stay at home, while others weigh the new offered options and decide it's worth the greater risk of catching the virus in exchange for what that extra pay will enable him and his family to provide for. Part of the cost would include being more vigilant in managing one's life away from work to minimize passing on the virus to others around them at home.

This way, each person can weigh things for himself, given his own circumstances as income earner, parent, spouse, son or daughter and make the choice that seems best for them, while not standing in the way or dictating what is right for anyone else. This seems far more reasonable and rational than the sledgehammer technique of the government's command and control system.

By its very nature, the government planners and their top-down planning method cannot know, appreciate, or incorporate all the nuanced details and bits of knowledge and information that makes each person's choice not only "right" for them, but that ends up freeing people up to go about doing what are the "right" things as reflected in the market demands and prices of what is needed most urgently by others in society, as well as where and when.

The anecdotal story about the origin of the term "laissez-faire," is that in 1681, the French minister of finance, Jean-Baptiste Colbert, asked a group of businessmen what the government could do to assist them, and one of them replied, "Leave it to us," that is, leave the marketplace alone to the free, peaceful and honest productions and trades of the participants on the supply and demand sides of a free market.

That is what the government should have done from the start in the face of the coronavirus crisis, and should introduce as quickly and thoroughly as possible right now, because its own central plans over the people and production of society are dragging the entire economy and society into a terrible economic downturn that will create very serious dislocations, shortages, lost jobs, and bring economic ruin to multitudes of Americans.

All that is needed to be done and should be done, even in this coronavirus crisis, is to leave people free to make their own choices and allow the free market to work its miracle of fulfilling the urgent demands of the moment to save lives, supply very needed goods and services, and find profitable ways of keeping those goods flowing and jobs existing to maintain as best as possible our standards of living.

AFTERWORD

A mere seven days after the completion of this manuscript, the world has become difficult to identify. Over two billion people are believed to be under government quarantine. Job losses are skyrocketing, with the US having just experienced a record number of unemployment claims in one week. School years, graduations, weddings, funerals, and other commonplace social events have been canceled well into the tens of thousands. And a $2.2 trillion stimulus package has been dwarfed by scores of emergency programs being extended by the Federal Reserve, which initially promised support for markets in amounts exceeding $4 trillion; that, failing to calm markets, was soon ratcheted up with pledges of quantitative easing measures described as "unlimited" in size and scope. What started as a run for toilet paper has become a nationwide stampede into physical gold, firearms, and properties in rural areas.

In the end, after all this incredible disaster has done its worst to destroy hope and civilized life, the lesson should be clear: this entire fiasco should have been left to the medical professionals to address in cooperation with markets, *sans* brutal intervention by regulators and politicians. Disease is complex and difficult. Researchers have worked this realm for one hundred years and more, even since the ancient world. If there are solutions to be had, society, not the state, has the greatest hope of finding them. If information flows had stayed open, systems allowed to scale, and information widely distributed, we could have handled this with compassion, intelligence, and focus.

Instead, we stand before wreckage — imposed in no small part by the use of monolithic force. I dearly hope this is temporary and we will look back on where we are in disbelief.

Healing is an extension of human volition, specialization, and knowledge. Disease and despair are spread by stupidity, pride, and force. Will we learn? Let us look carefully, understand, and learn. And then, teach. And along with the lessons we pass along, the following message: never again.

Peter C. Earle
March 27, 2020

ABOUT THE EDITOR

Peter C. Earle is an economist and writer who joined AIER in 2018 and prior to that spent over 20 years as a trader and analyst in global financial markets at a number of firms and funds.

His research focuses on financial markets, monetary policy, virtual and cryptocurrencies, and issues in economic measurement. He has been quoted in *The Wall Street Journal*, *Reuters*, *NPR*, and in numerous other publications

Pete holds an MA in Applied Economics from American University, an MBA (Finance), and a BS in Engineering from the United States Military Academy at West Point.

ABOUT AIER

The American Institute for Economic Research in Great Barrington, Massachusetts, was founded in 1933 as the first independent voice for sound economics in the United States. Today it publishes ongoing research, hosts educational programs, publishes books, sponsors interns and scholars, and is home to the world-renowned Bastiat Society and the highly respected Sound Money Project. The American Institute for Economic Research is a 501c3 public charity.

Made in the USA
Coppell, TX
02 April 2020